Fix it in a Flash

25 Common Home Repairs and Improvements

JODI MARKS with STEVE SCHULTZ

B
BETTERWAY HOME
CINCINNATI, OHIO
www.fwmedia.com

READ THIS IMPORTANT SAFETY NOTICE

To prevent accidents, keep safety in mind while you work. Use the safety guards installed on power equipment; they are for your protection. When working on power equipment, keep fingers away from saw blades, wear safety goggles to prevent injuries from flying wood chips and sawdust, wear hearing protection and consider installing a dust vacuum to reduce the amount of airborne sawdust in your woodshop. Don't wear loose clothing, such as neckties or shirts with loose sleeves, or jewelry, such as rings, necklaces or bracelets, when working on power equipment. Tie back long hair to prevent it from getting caught in your equipment. People who are sensitive to certain chemicals should check the chemical content of any product before using it. The authors and editors who compiled this book have tried to make the contents as accurate and correct as possible. Plans, illustrations, photographs and text have been carefully checked. All instructions, plans and projects should be carefully read, studied and understood before beginning construction. Due to the variability of local conditions, construction materials, skill levels, etc., neither the author nor Betterway Home Books assumes any responsibility for any accidents, injuries, damages or other losses incurred resulting from the material presented in this book. Prices listed for supplies and equipment were current at the time of publication and are subject to change.

METRIC CONVERSION CHART

TO CONVERT	TO	MULTIPLY BY
Inches	Centimeters	2.54
Centimeters	Inches	0.4
Feet	Centimeters	30.5
Centimeters	Feet	0.03
Yards	Meters	0.9
Meters	Yards	1.1

Distributed in Canada by Fraser Direct
100 Armstrong Avenue
Georgetown, Ontario L7G 5S4
Canada

Distributed in the U.K. and Europe by David & Charles
Brunel House
Newton Abbot
Devon TQ12 4PU
England
Tel: (+44) 1626 323200
Fax: (+44) 1626 323319
E-mail: postmaster@davidandcharles.co.uk

Distributed in Australia by Capricorn Link
P.O. Box 704
Windsor, NSW 2756
Australia

Visit our Web site at www.fwmedia.com. Other fine Betterway Home books are available from your local bookstore or direct from the publisher.

13 12 11 10 09   5 4 3 2

Library of Congress Cataloging-in-Publication Data available upon request from the publisher.

ACQUISITIONS EDITOR: David Baker-Thiel (david.thiel@fwmedia.com)
SENIOR EDITOR: Jim Stack (jim.stack@fwmedia.com)
DESIGNER: Brian Roeth
PRODUCTION COORDINATOR: Mark Griffin
PHOTOGRAPHER: Steve Schultz
ADDITIONAL PHOTOGRAPHY: Kate Schultz
ILLUSTRATIONS: Jim Stack
VIDEOGRAPHY: Black Box Media

fw media

ABOUT THE AUTHORS

About Jodi:

Born in Rome, Georgia, Jodi Marks had construction in her blood from the beginning. During her summers growing up, Jodi would "walk the job" with her dad on his different building sites, making sure everything was in order. After completing a degree in Psychology at the University of South Carolina, Jodi went to work for her father's construction company as project manager. While working construction by day, she began taking film classes at night and doing commercial/industrial work around the Atlanta area.

Jodi's love of theatre and her blueprint knowledge collided in 1997 when a call came from Home and Garden Television (HGTV) selecting her to co-host the series *Fix It Up!* Other HGTV credits include *Home Watch, Great Fall Fix Up* and *Blitz Build 2000*. In 2002, Jodi co-hosted *Southern Home by Design* for Turner South. In 2003, TBS brought Jodi on board as construction expert for the weekly series *The Man Made Movie*. In 2008, Jodi joined the team of *Today's Homeowner with Danny Lipford*.

When she's not shooting in the studio or on location, she can be found taking time out with her family to enjoy camping, fishing, and the great outdoors. Visit her web site at: www.jodimarks.com.

About Steve:

Steve has always loved adventure and creating things: radio-controlled airplanes, sports, drawing, painting, writing and theater — but especially fishing. His hobbies grew into photography, documentaries, fly fishing, trekking and home improvement. He started framing homes for his father's company at age 12. He played football at Colorado State University (Go Rams!) and after school sailed professionally for six years as a captain, travelling from Maine to Bermuda, through the Caribbean and down to Venezuela.

While sailing, film and video caught his attention while serving as the private captain for Hollywood producer Arne Glimcher (*Legal Eagles, Gorillas in the Mist, The Mambo Kings*, and more). He attended San Diego State University for his M.A. in Film and Communications and was awarded the KPBS Reeves Fellowship. He worked with KPBS for nearly five years as a videographer, writer, director and producer, while teaching television and film at SDSU.

He spent ten years as a corporate executive in internet technologies, and occasionally works as a consultant for startups to Fortune 500 companies. Steve has written for *Men's Journal*, *Fly Fishing America* and has been featured in *Entrepreneur* magazine.

ACKNOWLEDGEMENTS

From Jodi:

First I want to thank our editor, David Thiel, for believing in us, but also 'sensing' I could restrain my hyperness long enough to sit down and write a book! You've been so patient and so fun to work with. Thanks also to Brad Staggs and Beth Knott of Black Box Media. You are two of the best folks in video production and sheer joy to work with. I have to see the outtakes one day soon! I want to also thank my daughter, Hannah, for her infinite patience with me while writing this book. You are the star in my night sky and have become a pretty darn good cook, too! Thanks to my parents, Ray and Dotty. Mom, you gave me the courage and Dad, you lit the way. Lastly, I want to thank Steve. We've stretched and grown so much throughout this creative process. There isn't anything left for us to tackle together … including the kitchen sink. You inspire.

From Steve:

A big thanks to the four coaches and cheerleaders prompting me through this project; Brad and Beth of Black Box Media. David Thiel, captain, editor, photographer and man of all crafts and trades. Brad and David, the next time we shoot some video, I'll bring pom-poms for you both—the incessant humor served me well. Most importantly, I must give a very special thanks to Jodi. Your enthusiasm, passion, and vision was and is the cornerstone for not only this project, but the beauty you bring to everyone you touch (especially me). Hon, you simply make it happen! Finally, my little Kate, thanks for your understanding and helping your dad with the photography; you are now a published photographer.

Table of Contents

4 WALLS, FLOORS & CEILINGS

5 DOORS & WINDOWS

Welcome to Fix it in a Flash!

Steve and I are so excited to bring together some fun and easy projects that you can do around the house, or grab your significant other and tackle them as a team. Working on other folks' homes or on our own home, we have found that there are some basic repairs that just about everyone will encounter. With that in mind, we've specifically chosen 25 projects that anyone, no matter your DIY level, can take on. They don't require expensive or elaborate tools. If you can get your hands on a screwdriver, a hammer, a wrench, a pair of pliers or a saw, you can pretty much complete any of our top 25. Best of all, you can get them done in a few hours, or if needed, over the weekend.

When I was asked to write a home repair book, I was excited, but a bit hesitant. I had shot hundreds of hours of television shows showing folks how to do it. But sitting down and *writing* how to do it seemed a whole different story. Having worked with several co-hosts over the years, I thought it might make more sense to write this book with my real-life co-host,

Steve Schultz. He, like me, grew up in the family construction business, *but* he also was a published writer! This got me to thinking ... I could ask him to join me, then he could sit at the computer and write it while I walked around the room talking out loud, hands flying about, demonstrating each step of the projects we covered. What an awesome idea! We quickly learned that we both had a variety of experiences and anecdotes that we both wanted to share with the reader. That meant each of us would share in the writing. At first it was difficult for me to sit still. But once I got the hang of it, well ... here it is! I got baptized into Steve's world of writing. Not to be outdone, I, along with my editor, decided that a video should accompany the book. Thus, the tables were turned and Steve got a baptism by fire on being in front of the camera!

Steve and I both had a great time building this book and shooting the accompanying video. We hope you enjoy it as much as we enjoyed creating it.

Happy home improving!

1 HOME BASICS

THE VOCABULARY OF YOUR HOME

Owning a home is probably one of the greatest pleasures and is really a true sense of accomplishment for us adults. It's your space, reflective of your personality. You can be as clean or messy as you want, quiet or as loud as you want, simple or as bold in your décor as you want. But no matter what your habit or your style, one thing is consistent throughout each and every home … the structure and how it's typically built.

Getting to know the ins-and-outs of how your house is constructed is key. When it comes to repairs or improvements, this knowledge is paramount to the success or, let's face it, the failure of your projects. We're going to give you a quick lesson in the basics so you, too, can become the expert of your own domain.

Foundation

This is what your house is built on. You may have either a slab, crawl space, or basement, but whichever one you have, your house rests on footings that are buried in the ground and typically there are piers spaced throughout your crawl space or basement to give even, extra support to the weight of your home.

Footings

The type of soil will dictate how deep and wide your homes footing will have to be. Typically with good soil, not one with a lot of sand in it, a footing can be about 10" thick and 16" wide. Trenches are dug around the perimeter of the outside wall location of your house and a footing is poured all the way around. Your walls will be built on this strong support.

Sill Plate

Once your footings and foundation have been put in place, the framing of the house begins. First thing up are the sill plates made from 2 × 6 pressure-treated lumber that is anchored into the foundation.

Rim Joist Boards

These are 2 × 8's or 2 × 10's, vertically attached to the sill plate. The floor joists attach to the box they create.

Floor Joists

These are 2 × 8's or 2 × 10's, whichever ones your rim joists are, and they are the bones of your floor. You use joists hangers to attach each end of the floor joist to the rim boards. They are spaced 16" on center of each joist.

Subflooring or Decking

These are sheets of ¾" plywood. They are firmly attached to the floor joists and this is floor base you will be walking on later, of course, after you put down carpet, tile or hardwood planks.

Bottom Plate

This is the bottom part of your wall construction that is attached to your subfloor or decking. They can be 2 × 4's in places where its warm climate, or 2 × 6's if your house is located in colder areas.

Wall Studs

Same size as your Bottom Plate, either 2 × 4 or 2 × 6, these are attached vertically to create your wall structure. They are spaced usually 16" on center, but in some older homes you find that they are 24" on center. Their height will be determined by how high you want your finished ceiling height to be, either 8, 9, or 10 feet tall. Older homes I have been in have 12 to 14 feet high ceilings.

Top Plate

Same as the Bottom Plate and Wall Studs in dimension, it acts as a cap at the top of the Wall Studs to tie it all in and support your walls.

Ceiling Joists

These are usually 2 × 8's or 2 × 10's and I have even seen 2 × 12's depending on how many floors there are that need to be supported in the house. They tie the walls all together, are hung just like floor joists are using joists hangers and are typically 16" on center.

Rafters or Trusses

Depending on how your architect designed your house, you could either have trusses that were constructed in a warehouse and shipped to your location during construction, or your roof could have been "stick built" which means that the roof line is built on site one piece of lumber at a time. The trusses, or rafters, are the frame and support of your roof.

Sheathing

This is the plywood used, usually 4 × 8 sheets that are attached all around your house to the Wall Studs and Rafters to create the "skin" of your house.

House Wrap

This is the thin layer of protection you lay over the sheathing. You literally wrap it around your house to make sure it is well protected from the elements outside, to increase air and water resistance, and provide better protection against water and moisture problems. Some builders still prefer the old way of wrapping your home with felt construction paper.

Finished Siding

The homes' outside finish: Brick or stone, wood siding, vinyl siding, or fiber-cement siding.

Roofing Shingles

Most commonly used are the asphalt shingles due to their economic value and their life span. Clay tiles are also another form of roofing material as are cedar shingles and yes, metal ones. Each have their own strengths and can range from very affordable to very expensive depending on your budget.

ESSENTIAL TOOLS

It's time for me to come clean. I have an addiction. I love tools. I can't help it. I can still recall the smell of my dad's metal toolbox that he kept in the pantry off the kitchen. I would find myself rooting around in there trying to make sense of this or that tool. Everything was cool. I didn't have much exposure at that time to power tools. Everything of my dad's was hand-operated. Screwdrivers, small saws, pliers, folding measuring sticks. That's right, a wooden, folding measuring stick that messed up my precise measurement if it fell on the joint. Thank goodness tools have come a long way since I was a kid. Improvement on a good thing is well, a good thing. Now projects get done faster, safer, and are, in my humble opinion, more enjoyable. Depending on your project, you may need some specialty tools designed specifically for your task at hand. We'll cover those specific tools as they apply to each project. But the list at left is a good place to start when stocking your own work shop, even if your "shop" has to fit in a metal toolbox in your pantry like my dad's.

NICE TO HAVE

If you want to step it up a notch, you can always find great and useful additions to your basic tools. If your budget will allow, it's always a good idea to invest in a better-made, more reputable tool manufacturer that will stand by their products. There are some knock-off brands out there that might save you some coin right now, but in the long run you may pay double, if not more, when it needs to be replaced in one or two years. My suggestion is to always read up on a tool before you take the leap. The internet is a rare friend; one that likes to be used! So do it! Research, research, and then research some more. Try to avoid impulsively buying big ticket tools as you pass the tool section in your hardware store. I have to fight this, too, so I know how it goes. I could go on and on with a list of power tools that are fun to have. If you are going to do more than your fair share of projects around the house, then of course, power is better: i.e. powered nailers, bigger power saws, heavy-duty power drills and sanders. At left is a good jumping off point in the power tool direction that will help make even your basic to intermediate home repair projects go faster and more efficiently.

HIRING A CONTRACTOR

Since the beginning of my career in home improvement for television, it has pretty much been the focus of each show to give you some good information so you can tackle different projects around your home on your own. I, like you, enjoy feeling the sweat on my brow and my calloused hands hard at work. But,

you know, sometimes a project, no matter how badly you would like to take it on, is just too time consuming or daunting for you to do yourself. And you know what? That's okay!

Doing home improvement is not a contest that you have to win to prove your mettle to your spouse, your neighbor, or the person down at your local hardware store. The bottom line is that you have got to be confident before you rip out that sink or shut off that break switch that you are up to the "hassle" of home improvement. I have never heard a DIYer say their projects went off completely without a hitch. Even the pros race down to the hardware store two or three times in one day to get that part they need to finish the job.

Just remember this: it is home *improvement.* If it doesn't improve your mental wellbeing to start and finish a project, no matter how small, then I say don't put yourself through it. Call a licensed contractor. Nothing would make me sadder than to know that you jumped in unsure and half way through had to call someone to finish it up. They will know that you are "desperate" now and they just might take you for a bigger financial ride than if you had them quote the project in the first place.

I know doing it yourself can save you the labor charges involved in a project, but again, if the stress is too much for you or your family, it's not worth it. And your sanity is priceless.

2 ELECTRICAL

Yes, I know, the word "electrical" makes just about anyone nervous enough to pull out the phonebook and call the first electrician in the yellow pages instead of trying to tackle the simplest of wiring projects. Admittedly, when I purchased my first home, built in 1950, I was a bit more cautious since I knew the wiring was, at that time, over 40 years old. Let's face it, it doesn't matter if you are Joe and Judy DIYer or the guy and girl on that home improvement show, electricity makes people nervous when working around it. And rightfully so.

The good news is once you understand the basic components of electricity, you too, can take on some of the more fundamental projects. Nowadays, our homes have various types of wiring. Older homes sometimes have dated wiring that has never been updated, whereas some newer homes are wired for the future. If you are in doubt as to what type of wiring you're working with or feel uncomfortable moving forward in your project, by all means play it safe and call a certified electrician.

However, you can easily develop confidence to tackle electrical projects by understanding the basics of how electricity is brought in and controlled in your house.

Knowledge Is Power — Literally

Steve and I love the game show, *Jeopardy*. We try to tune in every evening and see who'll be master of trivia. I also love to share tidbits of information, trivial or otherwise. So here's your trivia question for the chapter: How does the power get to your outlets and switches in the first place?

It all starts at the Power Plant. A huge electrical generator spins to create electrical current. To make the generator spin, some regions of the country use a water wheel, like those found in a hydroelectric dam. Some areas use solar energy or wind to turn the generator; others may use either diesel or gas fuel. A more common way to spin the energy-producing generator is with steam, produced either by natural gas, coal, or nuclear energy.

Once the power leaves the generator it heads to a transmission substation. There the electrical voltage is greatly increased, anywhere from 150,000 to 750,000 volts, so it can travel long distances over the transmission grid.

From the transmission grid, the power is converted to lower volts on a distribution grid at a power substation. It is then sent out on distribution lines where transformers on these smaller power poles reduce the voltage even further so it can safely enter into your home on a service drop line that passes through your meter into your home's service panel.

The service panel is your home's main terminal for getting that power to all the different switches and outlets. The panel contains various breakers or fuses that monitor the amount of power each receptacle receives. Too much power to a specific receptacle or switch and the breaker is tripped or the fuse is blown. This action cuts the current to that area and thus protects you and your house. You will see different numbers on the top of the breaker or fuse denoting what is the maximum amperage, or electrical flow (current), a particular switch or outlet can hold.

Mapping this electrical circuitry helps you develop an understanding of the power in your house and how it's controlled. By mapping out your electrical circuitry you will then have the confidence to tackle these projects and more.

Creating a Circuit Map

We fortunately had a great electrician work on our house renovation. As he installed our service panel, he took the time to label all of our breaker tabs. This eliminated the time consuming task of flipping each breaker on and off until you hear the yell saying that the power went off. Ugh. If you weren't that lucky, no worries. Mapping your outlet and switches is easy.

First, draw a layout of your home. We have two service panels in our house, so we created a layout for each panel. This layout doesn't have to be to scale just make sure you account for every outlet, fixture and appliance. Once you complete your layout, recruit your partner, friend, neighbor or your kid to be your "eyes" in each room.

Remember, some room outlets and fixture switches located on the same wall or area may be controlled by the same breaker, so it's a good idea to have a radio or blow dryer plugged in to see if power is cut off at the outlet the same time power is cut to a specific fixture. Once correctly identified, note these on your layout and label each outlet or switch with its corresponding breaker number.

Once you label everything, transfer that information to the inside label on your service panel for quick reference. Then post your

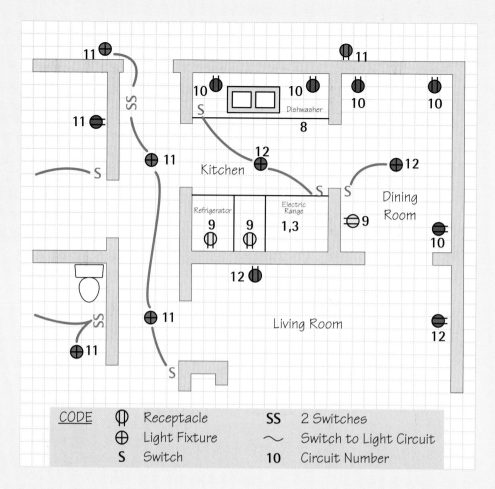

CODE				
⌀	Receptacle	**SS**	2 Switches	
⊕	Light Fixture	∼	Switch to Light Circuit	
S	Switch	**10**	Circuit Number	

layout next to the service panel for a more detailed reference. It's a good idea to cover the layout with clear contact paper to protect it from moisture or wear and tear.

Electrical Tips & Hints:

House wiring is measured in gauges. Oddly enough, as the number increases, the actual size or thickness of the wire decreases. So 10-gauge wire is actually thicker or larger than 18-gauge wire. Most of the wires you will encounter for your standard 120volt switches, outlets and fixtures will be either 12-gauge to 14-gauge.

When replacing an outlet, depending on how that room was wired, you may have two black hot wires, two white neutral wires and two green ground wires attached to your old outlet. This means that your outlet falls in the middle of a wiring run. If an outlet in the same room has only one black, one white and one green wire, then it means that the outlet is at the end of the wiring run in that room. Both instances are connected the same way, black wire to brass terminal and white wire to silver terminal. However, for a middle-of-the-run outlet where you will have 6 total wires to connect, you connect each black hot wire to each brass terminal screw and each white neutral wire to each silver terminal screw. To properly ground both green grounding wires, join the two grounding wires coming from the receptacle box with a grounding pigtail — an extra three-inch piece of same gauge copper wiring — using a green wire nut and secure the pigtail to the green grounding terminal screw. If the receptacle box is metal, use an additional pigtail connected from the other joined grounding wires to the green grounding terminal screw inside the receptacle box.

When making any electrical connection, always use a wire connector, also called a wire

Grounded Duplex Receptacle

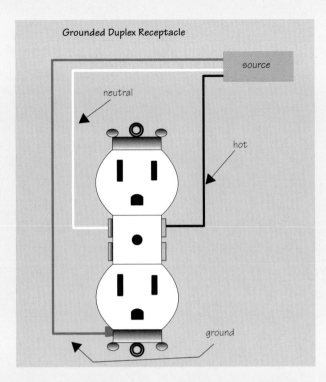

Outlet: Hot (black) wire to brass terminal screw, Neutral (white) wire to silver terminal screw, Ground (green or copper) wire to green terminal screw.

nut. They come in different sizes denoted by color. The wire nut size is relative to the wire gauge you are working with and its rating has a maximum to a minimum range. Only use a green wire nut when connecting ground wires together, other wire nuts are not rated for this use and should not be substituted.

Switch Loop Diagram

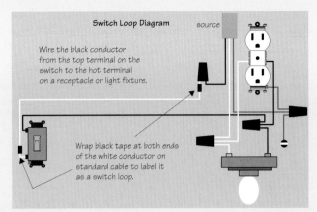

Wire the black conductor from the top terminal on the switch to the hot terminal on a receptacle or light fixture.

Wrap black tape at both ends of the white conductor on standard cable to label it as a switch loop.

Switch: Both Black and White wires are considered Hot. TIP: tape a piece of black electrical tape on white wire to denote that it is Hot.

Rheostat Wiring

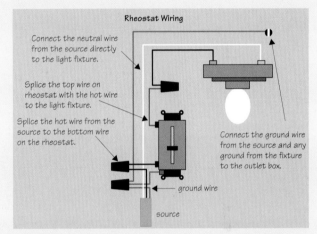

Connect the neutral wire from the source directly to the light fixture.

Splice the top wire on rheostat with the hot wire to the light fixture.

Splice the hot wire from the source to the bottom wire on the rheostat.

Connect the ground wire from the source and any ground from the fixture to the outlet box.

ground wire

source

Dimmer Switches: Hot (black) wire to Hot (black) wire or Hot (red) wire to Hot (black) wire, Neutral (white) wire to Neutral (white) wire, and Ground (green) wire to Ground (green) wire.

WIRE NUT GUIDE

COLOR	Minimum Gauge	Maximum Gauge	Max # of wires
Red	14	10	4
Yellow	16	14	4
Orange	18	14	2
GreenFor Ground Wires Only			4

Lighting

LIGHTING DESIGN

Over the years, I have witnessed many lighting trends in home construction. Even growing up with a dad as a builder, most lighting options were from the overhead flush mount in the center of the room with a lamp or two thrown in for good measure. And I remember when track lighting with the big, bulky can lights was the entire rage.

Now, lighting is seen as a very important aspect of just plain comfortable living. Ceiling fans are installed without their light kits in lieu of recessed lights in each corner of the ceiling. Under mount cabinet lighting is a given and

I even admit to having the light in my kitchen pantry automatically come on whenever I open the door.

If you're designing a house, now's the time to really think about what you want to accomplish with your lighting design. If you like to read in bed (like I do), then having direct lighting recessed lights over each side of the bed is a great idea. If you need more light in your bathroom than just a light mounted above the mirror, then adding wall scones on either side of the mirror, or actually attaching them to the mirror may be just the ticket. I even found that having a single mount ceiling fixture with three independent, directional light cans works perfectly in my closet so I can adjust each can to point right where I need it most.

If you're going to replace an old fixture for an updated and more serviceable light, you can bargain hunt all day long. If it costs a bit more to get what you really need, then do it and save somewhere else in your remodeling budget.

REPLACE A LIGHT FIXTURE

THERE ARE SEVERAL REASONS FOR replacing your light fixture. And if you have visited your local home improvement store lately, you know there are so many new styles and finishes for lighting. One of the main reasons for replacing a fixture is that it's now outdated. Brass finishes, for at least now, are a thing of the past. Now you can have oil rubbed bronze, pewter, brushed nickel, copper, or polished silver.

You can alter the look of a room just by changing a light fixture. So whether you have outdated fixtures and it is time to redecorate, or you're ready for the usefulness of a combination light and ceiling fan, replacing a light fixture is a great electrical project you can cut your teeth on and the changes can be very dramatic, yet inexpensive.

Most of the steps for replacing a light fixture also apply to ceiling fans or wall fixtures, such as a sconce. Make sure you review the manufacturer's instructions that came with your fixture; there may be special instructions for a mounting strap or plate that is specific to your fixture.

ELECTRICAL

Replace a Light Fixture

TIME: 30 minutes for basic fixture

EFFORT LEVEL: Basic

TOOLS AND MATERIALS:
- Screwdrivers—Flat head and Phillips
- Needle nose pliers
- Wire cutters or wire strippers
- Wire nuts
- Ladder
- Expandable hanger brace (if needed)

TROUBLESHOOTING: Examine the housing box and make sure it is securely attached to the ceiling joists on each side. If any doubt exists that the housing box may not hold the new fixture, you will need to install an expandable hanger brace or ceiling fan brace. These braces are installed through the ceiling opening. Shore them up against the ceiling joists. It's under $20 bucks and the ounce of prevention is well worth the pound of remedy.

ELECTRICAL TIP   The replacement and installation steps are the same for an indoor fixture or outdoor fixture. Note that outdoor fixtures must be designed for outdoor exposure. Also, make sure any fixtures going in a damp place like a bathroom are designed for moisture exposure. Otherwise, you will have corrosion buildup over time that will damage your new fixture.

1 Turn off the power to the fixture at the breaker or fuse box.

2 Remove the lightbulbs from the existing light fixture. If you'll be using them in your new fixture, set them aside in a safe location (well away from where you're working).

3 Remove the glass bells from the light fixture. Most bells are attached using three thumb screws at the top of the light. Hang on to the bell as you unscrew all three screws. Unscrewing one isn't enough to release the bell.

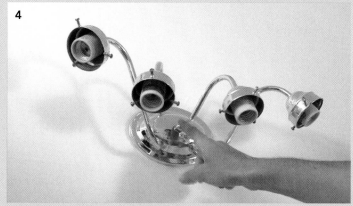

4 Wall light fixture vary by manufacturer, but most attach to the mounting plate by one or more cap nuts that can be simply unscrewed with your fingers. Again, hang on to things; when the nut comes loose, so will the light fixture!

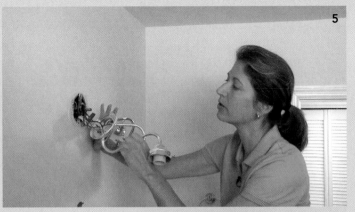

5 Carefully pull the fixture from the wall. The wires are still attached (or should be) and while the fixture can probably hang by the wires, if some of the wires are loose, it could drop unexpectedly.

6 Locate the black, white and green wires from the housing box, and confirm that the power is off. Use a circuit tester and test the wires connected to the fixture. If there is no power, proceed on.

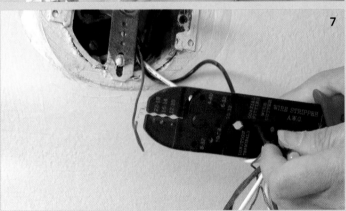

7 Rather than fight with the old wiring, it's just as simple to cut away the wires, as close to the old fixture as possible, to leave plenty of wire in the housing box. This will make attaching the new fixture easier.

8 More likely than not, there will be a mounting plate attached to the housing box. Remove the screws holding this plate in place and remove it.

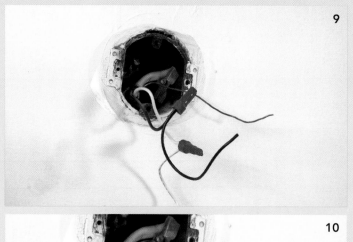

9 Take a close look at the wires in the box. If the wires are kinked or damaged, cut off the damaged wire. In our case shown here, extra wiring had been added with wire nuts to extend the length. We have plenty of wire in the box, so we're going to just remove these "jumpers" and the wire nuts.

10 With the wires exposed, check the tips. If they're in good shape, then move on to the next step. If they're crimped, twisted, or the exposed wire is less than 1/2" long, cut away the end and use wire strippers to strip the sheathing to expose a 1/2" of new wiring.

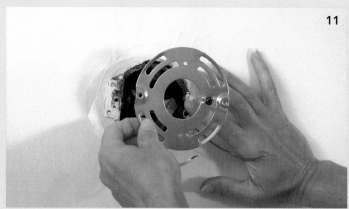

11 Your new light likely comes with a new mounting plate. The one shown here is a universal plate allowing an easy fit to most housing boxes.

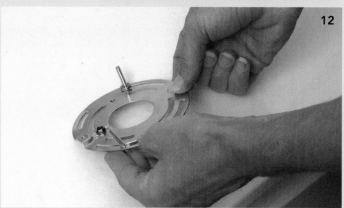

12 To match the existing box, new threaded bolts are attached to the mounting plate. These are necessary in our case because the housing box is mounted in the wall at an angle, and our new fixture would hang crooked otherwise. Nuts thread over the bolts to hold them in place.

13 The new mounting plate is then mounting in the housing box, using the existing screws. Align the new threaded bolts so they're level.

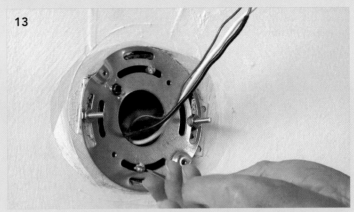

14 With the plate mounted, tuck back some of the extra wire into the box. It's more easily done at this step...

15 Attach the wires from the new fixture to the existing wiring in the box. If you've got a friend handy, someone holding the new fixture is a help. If not, a step ladder will do in a pinch to support the light fixture. Attach black-to-black, white-to-white and bare copper (the ground wire) to the same.

16 With the wires attach, push as much of the wire back into the box as possible. Then bring the new fixture up to the mounting plate and slip the mounting bolts through the holes in the fixtures base plate.

17 Just like on the old fixture, cap nuts hold the new fixture in place. Screw the first one in place far enough to hold the fixture in place, then screw on the second (and any others if necessary). Screw the nuts in place to hold the fixture snug to the wall at this point.

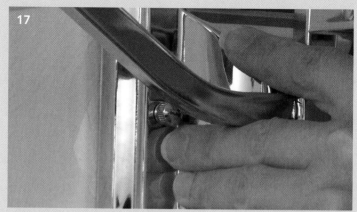

18 While you can "eyeball" the fixture to decide if it's level, if you have a real level handy, why not use it? When the fixture is level, tighten the cap screws to hold the fixture tight against the wall.

19 All that's left is to mount the new glass bells and put the new light bulbs in place.

20 Turn on the breaker and take a look at your new fixture. This thirty-minute project can make a dramatic difference in your bathroom, or any room!

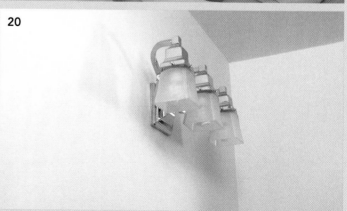

Ceiling Fan Brace

SUPPORT THE WEIGHT

Whether you're adding a chandelier in your dining area, or a ceiling fan in the kid's bedroom, it's always nice to have electric run to the position already. A common mistake, however, is assuming that the electrical box mounted in the ceiling will support the weight of the fixture.

A standard electric box may be simply nailed to the side of a ceiling joist and isn't designed to support the weight of a heavy lighting fixture.

Not to worry! A very handy after-market accessory is available from a few manufacturers that replaces the existing electrical box with a support brace that expands and attaches to the joists.

You may be required to do a little drywall work (moving the box location), but to add the peace of mind of knowing that your ceiling fan will stay on the ceiling is worth a little extra work.

INSTALL A CEILING FAN

I REMEMBER THE FIRST TIME I INSTALLED A CEILING FAN. I WAS 25, and 6 months pregnant with my daughter. Alone one afternoon, trying to get the nursery all set up for her arrival, it occurred to me that a ceiling fan would be just the right touch to her room.

I raced down to the hardware store, picked out a pretty white one, lugged it into her room and had it up by that evening.

Looking back, I have to admit I wouldn't recommend working on a ladder and lifting a not-so-light ceiling fan into place while pregnant. But, installing a ceiling fan is as straight forward as installing any lighting fixture, the only difference is its assembly and weight.

Make sure that you have someone on hand to help you lift the fan onto the hook of the ceiling plate or the mounting bar if your model has that. Also, if you are taking down an existing fixture and replacing it with a heavy ceiling fan, make sure you have reinforced the outlet box in the ceiling with a support brace.

The project shown here is replacing an existing ceiling fan. Essentially the same steps would be required to replace a ceiling light with a ceiling fan. If there is no existing fixture, you'll need to start with a new reinforced electrical box and run some wiring, which, honestly, means it's time to call an electrician.

Ceiling Fan

TIME: About one hour

EFFORT LEVEL: Moderate

TOOLS AND MATERIALS:
- Screwdrivers—Flat head and Phillips
- Pliers or wrench
- Power Drill
- Wire nuts (if not provided with fan)
- Ladder

1 As with any electrical project, start by making sure the power is off at the breaker. Our existing ceiling fan has a neat decorative trim piece hiding the mounting screws for the fan. Yours may not have this, in which case you'll be looking at the screws and step 2 is the one for you. If no screws are obvious, look for a way to remove the trim strip.

2 Unscrew the screws holding the cover housing from the existing fan. Nothing heavy should come loose, just a cover, but still, work cautiously.

3 Nothing came loose in our case, because the housing was sealed to the ceiling with paint. A utility knife took care of that issue quickly.

4 Now the housing will come loose and hang down from the ceiling, exposing the wires inside.

5 With the wires exposed, you should be able to remove the wire nuts, disconnecting the old fixture. For peace of mind, you may want to get your tester and check to make sure the electricity is off to the fixture first.

6 With the wires disconnected, you can grasp the fan fixture and lift it free of the mounting bracket. It may be a little heavy, so having a friend handy to help is smart. You may also want to consider removing the fan blades to make it easier to handle.

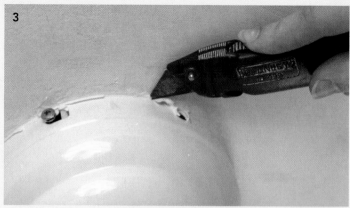

3

4

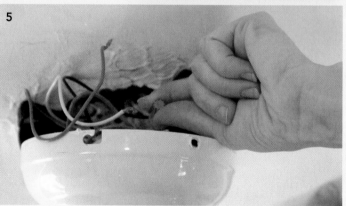

5

6

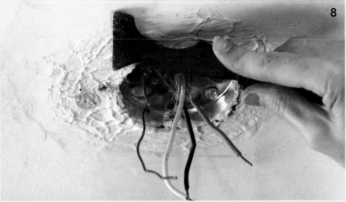

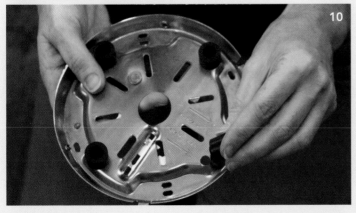

7 If you're replacing an existing ceiling fan (like us) there will be a hanging bracket mounted to the electrical box. Most are specific by manufacturer, so you'll need to remove the old bracket. If you're mounting a fan to an existing light fixture, this is the time to make sure the existing electrical box will support the weight of a ceiling fan. Follow your fan's instructions for this step.

8 With the bracket removed, I'm using a putty knife for remove some built-up plaster and paint on the ceiling that will keep our new fan from seating properly against the ceiling.

9 There are lots of parts with any celing fan kit. It's smart to lay everything out and familiarize yourself with the pieces.

10 The first piece I need to get better acquainted with is the mounting plate. This model requires four rubber bumpers that keep the fan from rocking when spinning. These are simply slipped in place on the mounting plate.

11 Back on the ladder, tidy up the wires leading from the electrical box and feed them through the appropriate hole in the mounting plate.

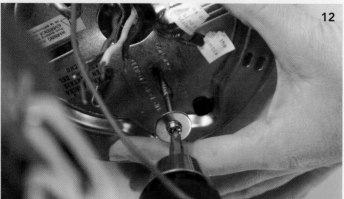

12 The plate itself then screws into the appropriate holes in the electrical box.

13 Our fan is a flush-mount model, so the next step is to secure the mounting stud to the fan motor. If yours is a post-mounted model, you'll also need to attach a mounting to the motor at this time, but it will also include the post.

14 Whether flush-mount or post-mount, a trim ring will rest against the ceiling. Most need to slip over the wiring at this point, or it'll be tough to add later!

15 Our fan includes a grounding plate that screws inside the ceiling housing.

16 With the wires fed through both the grounding plate and housing, screw the plate to the mounting stud already in place on the motor.

17 With many fan kits, the wires come with the insulation already stripped back the appropriate distance for easy connecting.

18 If your kit doesn't have pre-stripped wires, remove about ½" of insulation from the end of each wire using a pair of wire strippers.

19 Making the wiring connections at the ceiling can be a challenge. Many ceiling fan kits include a hook on the mounting plate to support the motor while you're making the wiring connections.

20 As you start to put the wires together, remember that like-color usually works. Black-to-black, white-to-white, and so on. I like to start with the ground wires, just to get them out of the way. A wire nut secures the connection.

21 Ground is attached, white wires are next ...

22 ... followed by the black connections.

19

20

21

22

23 With all the connections complete, tuck the loose wires as close to the mounting plate as possible. Once you lift the motor up to attach to the plate, you don't want to have to fight with wires, and you don't want to get one caught or pinched.

24 With the motor lifted into place, I just need to tighten a couple of screws to hold everything in place.

25 The decorative trim collar slips into place to hide those unsightly screws.

26 Next, it's time to get Steve in here. He fastened the blade brackets to the blades themselves. This particular fan kit includes rubber grommets to protect the wood of the fan blades, and also reduce noise. They simply slip into the holes in the blades.

27 Then it's a simple step to screw the blades to the mounting brackets.

28 It's usually two screws per bracket to attach the blades. We recommend leaving the first screw a little loose until the second screw is started, then tighten both.

29 We're adding a light kit to our fan. Three screws attach the light kit.

30 To run power to the light, it's a simple plug-in connection. I like that!

31 Lastly, the light kit base is screwed in place on the fan motor.

32 We're using compact fluorescent bulbs in our light fixture to save energy, and to keep from having to change light bulbs as often. Compact fluorescent bulbs can last up to three-times longer than standard incandescent bulbs.

33 Our frosted glass globe slides over the mounting stub and is screwed in place with a hand-tightened retaining knob.

REPLACE A LAMP SOCKET

FROM TIME TO TIME, LAMP FIXTURES JUST get worn out. We, or should I say "I", have a favorite lamp that sits on Steve's nightstand. I think I picked it up at a yard sale years ago. The trouble is, every now and then, it sputters out leaving Steve in the dark while he is reading in bed. He's ready to toss it. I can't live without it. So it was time for lamp surgery.

Turns our the lamp needs a new socket, and wouldn't you know; there are several different types of socket connections for lamps. Your socket may screw into place. Another one may snap into place. You may have a screw that secures it, or you may not. Regardless of which one you have, once you have removed the socket from its seat, you are ready to disconnect the old one and install the new one. And hey, if you are tired of having that type of switch on your socket, be it a pull chain, push-push switch, or twist switch, now is the time to change that, too.

ELECTRICAL

Lamp Socket

TIME: 30 minutes

EFFORT LEVEL: Basic

TOOLS AND MATERIALS:
- Screwdrivers — Flat head and Phillips
- Needle nose pliers
- Utility knife
- Wire cutters and strippers
- New socket

1 Here's a snap shot of all the tools we'll use. You'll notice we also have all our supplies ready to go. I've even included an extra cord, just in case. I hate making trips to the hardware store in the middle of a project!

2 And before we start, you'll need to unplug the lamp ... duh!

3 With the lamp shade and the light bulb removed, take a look at the socket you're replacing. If it screws down in place on the stem, unscrew it. If a small setscrew holds it in place, remove that and pull the socket free of the socket base.

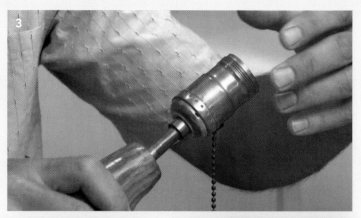

4 In our case, the socket snapped onto the socket base. Gently squeeze the socket body and rock it back and forth to release it from the socket base.

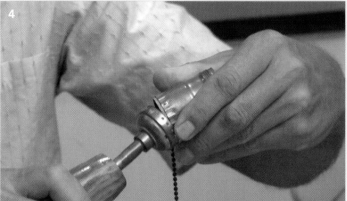

5 Slide off the socket shell and insulation cover to expose the terminal screws that hold the cord wires in place.

6 Using a screwdriver, loosen the terminal screws…

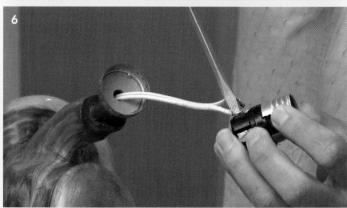

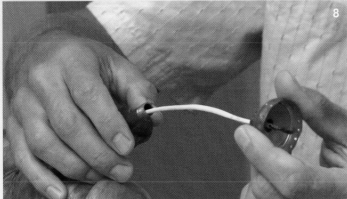

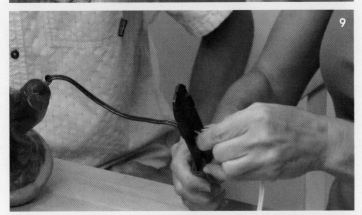

7 And disconnect the wiring from the old socket and inspect the exposed wiring. If it is badly crimped or fraying, trim it off with the wire cutters.

8 Remove the old socket base from the threaded rod of the lamp. Usually it is held in place with a setscrew or is screwed down on the threaded rod of the lamp.

9 Now we decided to replace our worn out, white cord with a new brown one. To learn more about that, jump to the next project. We trimmed the wire of the new brown cord, once it was fished through the lamp, about 12" to give us plenty to work with..

10 Feed the lamp cord through the new socket base…

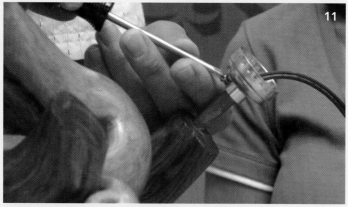

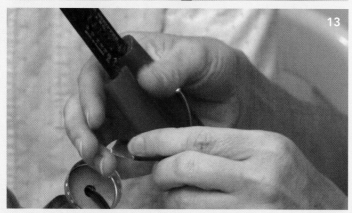

11 Attach the socket base to the threaded rod of the lamp either by screwing it down in place or by tightening the setscrew to hold it in place.

12 Steve was great at tying an Underwriter's Knot…all those years of fly-fishing!) For details on this knot, see page 43.

13 If after tying your knot the strands are too long, use your wire cutters to cut away the frayed part.

14 Then you will need to expose about ½" of the wire threads by using your wire strippers to pinch and then pull the sheathing off the ends.

15 Bend the exposed wire into a U shape and wrap the hot (smooth) wire around the brass terminal screw and the neutral (ribbed) wire around the silver terminal screw.

16 Tighten each terminal screw down with a screwdriver, making sure as your tighten them the wire doesn't pop out from underneath the screw head.

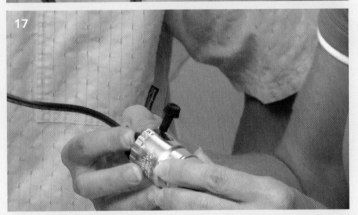

17 Slide the socket shell and insulation sleeve over the socket body. They should pretty much both stay together when sliding them back into place, but if not, the white insulation slides on first and then the outer metal shell.

18 From bottom of lamp, gently pull any excess cord through the lamp body allowing new socket to rest inside of new socket base. Snap, screw, or tighten down socket body into socket base and you are finished! Replace light bulb and lamp shade, plug lamp into receptacle and test out your great work.

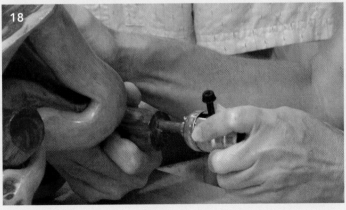

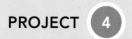

REPLACE A LAMP CORD

A GOOD FRIEND OF OURS ALWAYS SAYS, "There's nothing more permanent than a temporary fix." How true.

When it comes to damaged or frayed lamp cords, slapping a piece of electrical tape over the problem is NOT the cure ... we've seen it dozens of times and it's a fire waiting to happen. Change the cord. It is so easy. No more fire hazard or potential shock.

You can pick up a cord replacement kit at your local hardware store. They come in several color options and the plug is already attached.

ELECTRICAL

Replace a Lamp Cord

TIME: 20 minutes, or 15 minutes if you've had 2 cups of Steve's coffee

EFFORT LEVEL: Basic

TOOLS AND MATERIALS:
- Screwdriver
- Wire cutters and strippers
- Utility knife
- Needle nose pliers
- Electrical tape

1 Start by cutting off the plug with a pair of wire cutters or a sharp pair of scissors.

2 Prepare the new cord for use. Cut the cord length and give yourself a few extra inches.

A. Measure 3 inches from the end of the cord. Using the utility knife, slice the center groove, creating two separate strands.

B. Remove ¾ inch of insulation from both strands with the wire stripper.

C. Repeat the above process on the other end of the cord, unless you purchased a cord with the plug attached.

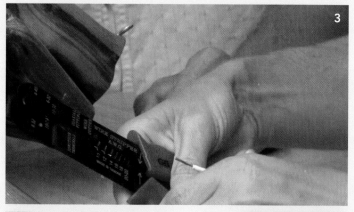

3 Using the wire strippers, expose about ½" of the wires on both strands.

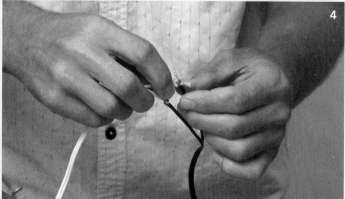

4 Join both cords together by wrapping the strands from the old cord to the strands of the new cord.

5 For additional strength, wrap a piece of duct tape over joined strands. Use a small enough piece to cover the wires, yet not too big to squeeze through the lamp rod and lamp base.

6 From the top of the lamp, gently pull the joined cords through the lamp. You may have to squeeze the tape to flatten it so it can pass through the lamp body. If there is a setscrew at the base of your lamp holding the cord, loosen it to allow the cord to move freely.

7 Pull the new cord all the way through the top, giving yourself about 12" of cord at the top to work with. We cut off the old cord at the taped end, giving us a fresh, undamaged end of our new cord.

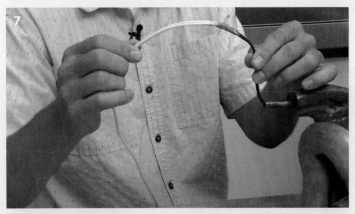

8 HOW TO TIE AN UNDERWRITER'S KNOT: Pull the strands apart and give yourself about 6" of wire length. Now you are ready to tie an Underwriter's Knot. An Underwriter's Knot adds support for the wire connections. This knot will absorb any sudden pulling or yanking of the cord that might otherwise cause the wires to disconnect from the terminal screws on the socket body.

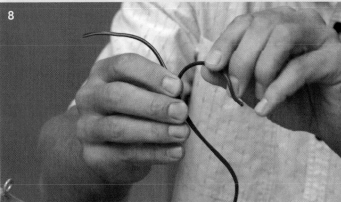

9 Take one strand and turn it downward and across the top of the cord to create a loop. Pinch it between your fingers to hold the loop in place.

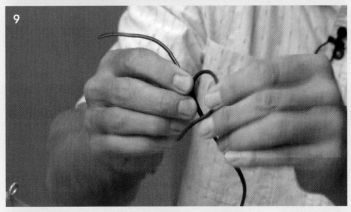

10 Take the other strand and turn it downward to make a loop.

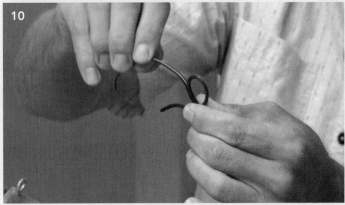

11 Thread the end of second strand through the loop of the first strand.

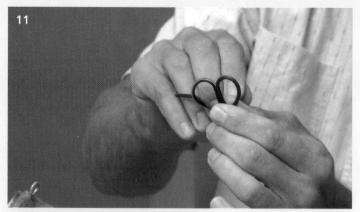

12 Feed the end of the first strand into the loop of the second strand.

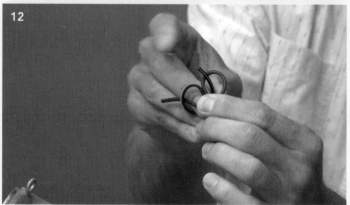

13 Gently pull the ends of both strands at the same time creating the perfect Underwriter's Knot.

14 Now you are ready to make the necessary connections of the wire strands to the new socket. To see how to make these connections, refer to the previous project.

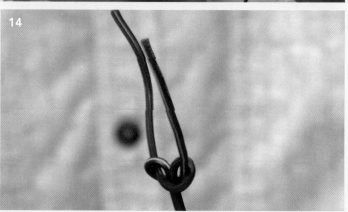

REPLACE A CORD PLUG

WE INHERITED SEVERAL HANDMADE pine lamps made by Steve's great-grandfather. Nearly every lamp needed the plugs replaced because of age, loose prongs, or they were cracked. Even if they worked they clearly were a safety hazard.

Cord plugs generally come in two types—round or flat-wire plugs. High-amperage appliances, like vacuum cleaners, irons, blow dryer, usually have round-plugs. Flat-plugs normally are attached to lamps, radios, clocks, and chargers. You can also use these steps to replace a worn out receptacle on the end of an extension cord.

ELECTRICAL

Replace a Cord Plug

TIME: 15 minutes

EFFORT LEVEL: Basic

TOOLS AND MATERIALS:
- Screwdrivers—Flat head and Phillips
- Needle nose pliers
- Wire cutters or wire strippers
- Replacement plug (matching old plug style — round or flat)
- Utility knife

TIPS AND HINTS:
- Cut off the plug you are replacing and take it with you to the store to make sure you are matching it with a similar plug.
- When replacing a plug, double check the cord to see what shape it's in. If it's showing signs of wear or has a tear in the sheathing, go ahead and replace it while you have the lamp out of commission.

ELECTRICAL TIP

QUICK-CONNECTING FLAT-WIRE PLUG:

1. Cut off the plug from the unplugged cord using the wire cutters.

2. Insert the cut end of the cord into the back of the new quick-connect plug and press down. Or, if you have the 2-piece style, place the end of the cord between the two pieces and clamp together. Ensure that the internal prongs pierce through the wire's insulation to make the connection with the wires in the cord.

3. Recheck all connections and confirm that they are secure. Test the cord by plugging it in. Do not make any adjustments when the plug is inserted in a receptacle.

1 Using a pair of wire cutters, cut off the damaged plug or receptacle at the end of the cord. Cut as close to the damaged piece as possible to ensure that you get as much cord length as the repair will allow.

2 If there is damage near the end of the cord as well, cut that away as well to have a good end of the cord to work with. Here the white wire is a flat cord and the black one is round. Both are in good shape and ready to go.

3 The new plug we have will be attached to the black round wire. It's a bit bulkier than a lamp plug since it goes to our vacuum.

4 Notice the ends of the two different plug/receptacle types. Like our wires, the black one is for a round wire and the white one is for a flat wire.

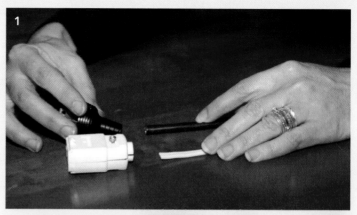

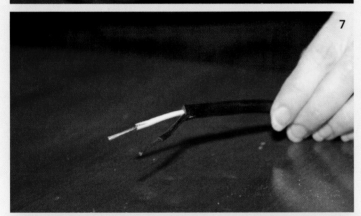

5 Starting on the round cord, we removed the outer sheathing with a utility knife. You can also use wire strippers or a cable ripper. You want to expose about 3" of the black and white wires inside the sheathing. You'll tie an Underwriters Knot in a minute and need to have enough wire to do so.

6 With your wire strippers, strip away about ¾" of the inner sheathing on both the black and white wires.

7 Some wires, once exposed, may either have a thick, solid copper wire or multiple, thin copper wires all bunched together. If they are the thin ones, twist the wires between your forefinger and thumb and shape them into a solid one.

8 Remove the prongs from the plug body and slide it over the cord. Be patient when removing the pronged top. It can be stubborn!

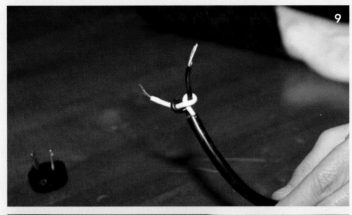

9 Tie that Underwriters Knot. To do this, refer to page 43 to see how easy this is to do.

10 With a pair of needle nose pliers, bend the ends of each wire into a U shape. We always bend the wires to go in a clock-wise direction so when we tighten the screws down clock-wise, the wires will keep their shape.

11 Place each wire under the terminal screw and secure them with your screwdriver. If each terminal screw is the same color, brass, then it doesn't matter which wire is attached to which terminal screw. If there is a brass and a silver screw, always attach the black wire to the brass screw and the white wire to the silver screw.

12 Snap the pronged top back into the plug body. Our new plug is attached to the old round cord and we are back in business!

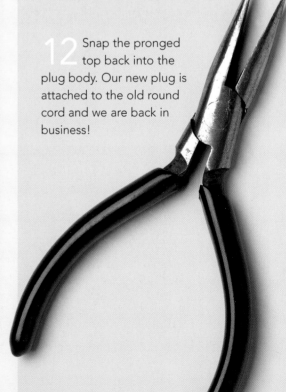

13 Now for our white, flat cord we are going to replace an extension receptacle to our end. Again, expose the copper wiring.

14 Remove the screw of the receptacle to open the receptacle body. Attach the wires to the terminal screws by bending the wire into a U and securing them under the screws.

15 We did not have to tie an Underwriters Knot for this application since the receptacle body provided a channel for the cord to rest inside the receptacle.

16 Once the screw is set back in place, the inner channel will hold the wires securely and your extension cord is all set to go!

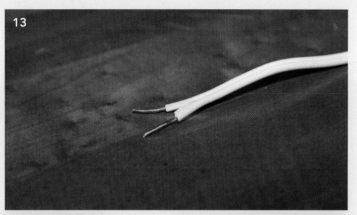

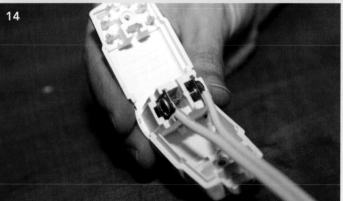

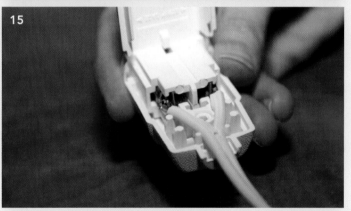

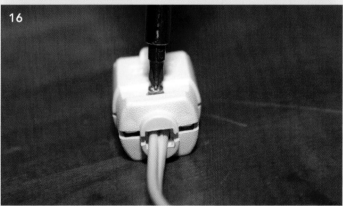

REPLACE A LIGHT SWITCH

THE GREAT THING ABOUT REPLACING A light switch is that both the white and black wires are hot. Therefore it does not matter if you place either wire at the top or bottom terminal (screw), both are correct.

Whether you have a damaged light switch, like in our case, or you just want to update your old one with a newer, cleaner looking one, this project is great primer to tackling your electrical DIY projects.

Replace a Light Switch

TIME: 15 minutes

EFFORT LEVEL: Basic

TOOLS AND MATERIALS:
- Screwdrivers—Flat head and Phillips
- Circuit tester
- Wire cutters
- Needle nose pliers
- New light switch (matching amperage and voltage of old switch)

1 If yours looks like ours, then it's time to replace it! Just make sure that you have turned the power off to the switch at the breaker box before going any further.

2 Once the power is off, remove the faceplate from the wall to expose the old switch.

3 We always recommend that you double check that the power if off. So using your circuit tester, place the prongs on the terminal screws of the light switch. If you get a red light or a warning, there is power still activating that switch! Double check that breaker!

4 Now that you know for sure there is no power there, (did we stress that enough?), use your screwdriver to remove the screws securing the switch to the switch box.

5 Pull the old switch out to expose all the wires back there. You may see black ones, red ones, or black/white swirl ones. Except for the green ground wire, these wires are all considered "hot" when the power is turned back on.

6 If you weren't able to reach the screws easily prior to removing the switch (or you just want to double check), use your tester to make sure.

7 With your screwdriver, loosen the terminal screws to release all the wires from under them.

8 Or, if your wires are attached to the old switch in the back, remove the wiring by pressing a flat head screwdriver into the slot below it to release it.

9 Double check that your new switch has the same amperage and voltage as your old one. This will be inscribed in the back. It's always a good idea to take your old with you when purchasing your new one to make sure it's the right replacement.

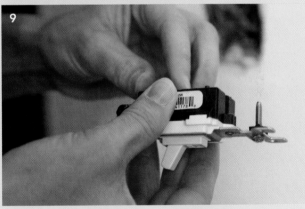

10 Attach the green, ground wire to the green tinted terminal screw usually found at the bottom of the switch.

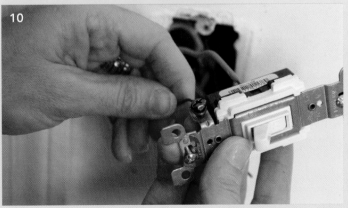

11 Sometimes that ground wire is a bit thick, so take a pair of needle nose pliers to shape the wire into a U and pinch it around the grounding screw.

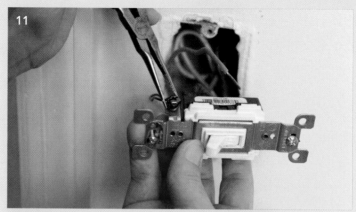

12 Using a screwdriver, tighten down the terminal screw. Here's a tip: Don't over-tighten the terminal screws because it may cause the wire to pop out from underneath the screw, breaking the power connection to the switch.

13 If you are going to wrap the wires around the terminal screws to make your connections, use the needle nose pliers to make the U-shape.

14 If you are going to make your connections by inserting the wires into the back of the switch, take your needle nose pliers and straighten out the wire.

15 To use the terminal screws, place the wire around the screw. Notice that the wire is wrapped around the screw in a clock-wise direction. This will ensure a proper connection once the screws are tightened down.

16 If you are going to use the slots in the back, simply push the straightened wire into the hole until you feel it click into place. Test its security by gently pulling on the wire.

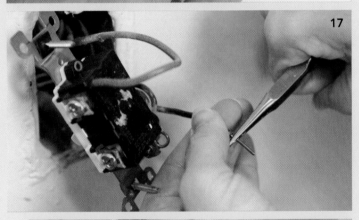

17 Now both the red wire and the black wire are hot, so you can connect either one on the upper and lower terminal of the switch. Straighten out or curl the other "hot" wire, in our case, the black one.

18 Since we are inserting them into the slots in the back, we pushed the wire into the back, making sure it clicked into place and was secure.

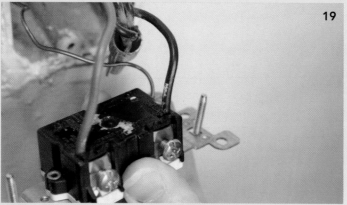

19 This is what the connections should look like when using the slots. Personally, we think this is the stronger connection. But either way is perfectly acceptable.

20 Gently push the wires and switch back into the switch box. You want to make sure that the switch is positioned correctly. You should be able to read the word "on" and "off". If not, you have the switch upside down.

21 Secure the switch to the switch box with the screws provided. Keep in mind that sometimes switches may not come with these longer screws, so always hold on the old screws in case.

22 We decided Kate, Steve's daughter, needed a fancier switch faceplate, so we picked up a pretty new one to go with her new switch. Put the cover in place, turn the power back on and test out your handy work! Good job!

INSTALL A DIMMER SWITCH

AH, DIMMER SWITCHES—ONE OF OUR favorite little tricks to add ambiance to any room. Installing a dimmer switch allows you to adjust the degree of lighting in the room. Whether it's for softening the harsh make-up lights around your bathroom mirror while you're trying to relax in the tub, or over your dining room table for that romantic dinner, dimmers really do give more bang for the buck to any fixture. They are not that expensive and very easy to install.

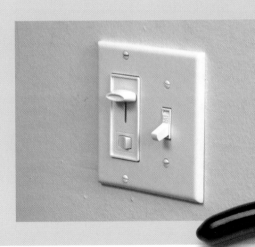

ELECTRICAL

Install a Dimmer Switch

TIME: 15 minutes

EFFORT LEVEL: Basic

TOOLS AND MATERIALS:
- Screwdrivers — Flat head and Phillips
- Voltage tester
- Needle nose pliers
- Wire cutters or wire strippers
- Wire nuts
- Dimmer switch
- New switch plate

DIMMER TIP Standard dimmer switches can't control all types of fixtures. Fixtures such as ceiling fans and fluorescent lights need special dimmer switches. Most dimmers are sold separately from their matching faceplate.

1 First and foremost, turn off the power at the breaker box to the light switch you are working on. If you have a fuse box, remove the fuse and set it aside.

2 Have all your tools set out and within reach to make the project go smoothly. One tool I use every time I am doing an electrical project is my circuit tester. It's an absolute must!

3 Remove the faceplate of the switch using your screwdriver. A good tip is to tape the tiny screws to the inside of the plate so you can find them later.

4 Remove the longer screws of the switch that secure it to the switch box. I also hang on to these in case my new switch does not come with new screws.

5 Without touching the wire connections on the side of the old switch, gently pull out the switch you are replacing. In our case, we had two switches there, but only wanted to make one of them a dimmer switch.

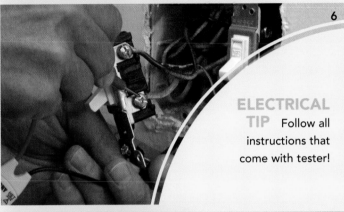

ELECTRICAL TIP Follow all instructions that come with tester!

6 With your invaluable circuit tester, touch both sides of the switch on the terminal screws to double check that the power is indeed turned off to the switch. If you get a red light or a warning light you still have power coming to that switch. Do not proceed! Try another breaker.

ELECTRICAL TIP Touching the tester to different parts of the switch may give you inaccurate readings.

7 If you have another switch at the location you are working like we do, check to make sure the power is killed at that switch too. You don't want to be working around a switch box that has any power coming to it.

DIMMER TIP Most people think that when they want to add a dimmer switch to a fixture that has two different switch locations, they need to install a 2-way switch. Actually, if a fixture has two or more switch locations controlling the light, it's called a 3-way switch and requires you to install a 3-way dimmer switch. If you want both locations to control the dimmer, you will have to purchase a dimmer switch that is designed specifically for that. It is referred to as a master-slave combination dimmer. It can be expensive, so if your budget is tight, install a 3-way dimmer switch in only one of the switch locations.

8 Once the coast is clear that the power is off at the switch or switches, use your screwdriver to loosen the terminal screws holding the wires.

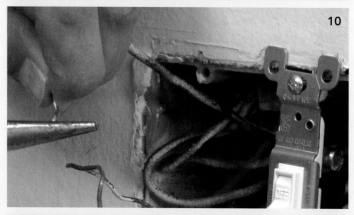

9 You may even have to use a pair of needle nose pliers to pry the wires away from the old switch. If the wires are connected directly into the back of the switch, use a flathead screwdriver and push it into the slots to release the wires.

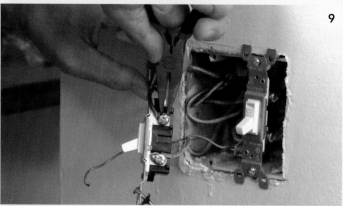

10 On a dimmer switch, there are three wires already attached for you to make the connections to the wires in the wall. You do not need to make a U-shape at the ends of the wires to wrap around terminal screws. In fact, you'll likely need to straighten the ends of the wires coming from the wall with a pair of needle nose pliers.

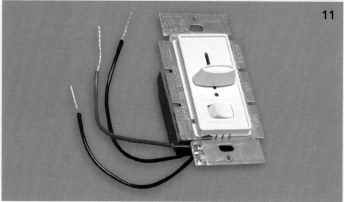

11 Remember, both wires coming from the wall are considered "hot", except, of course, the green one which is your ground wire. So it doesn't matter if your wires are black or red, whichever two wires that were connected to your old switch are the two that you are going to connect to the two "hot" wires attached to your dimmer.

12 To make the connections, take a hot wire from the wall and a hot wire from the dimmer and place them side by side. You can even wrap the exposed wires around each other, just make sure you wrap them in a clock-wise direction. Using a wire nut, twist it onto the exposed wires and turn it clock-wise until it stops. Do this for the other hot wire and the ground wire as well.

13 Gently, push all the wires back into the switch box making sure that the wire nuts do not become loose and twist off. This will break the connection and expose hot wires inside the switch box once the power is turned back on…and we don't want that!

14 Tighten down the screws that secure the dimmer switch to the switch plate. The slot may not be a perfect circle, it may offer you a bit of wiggle room to align the dimmer switch so you tweak it and make sure it is perfectly straight.

15 Turn the breaker back on or replace the fuse in the fuse box.

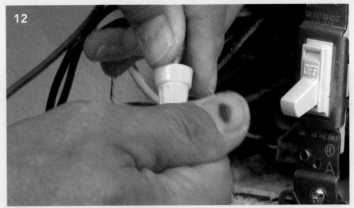

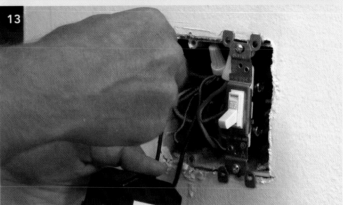

16 Test your dimmer switch. Make sure that the lights dim correctly. If they don't, turn the power back off and double check your connections. They may have come loose.

17 Everything is working fine, so we've got dimmer lighting for when we're just looking for a snack …

18 … and full lighting for when we're making a full dinner.

19 With our test complete, replace the faceplate made for the new dimmer. Most are sold separately, and they can come in a variety of styles and configurations depending on your situation.

The New Look of Dimmer Switches

Remember the push-and-turn dimmer switches? They're still around, but rather than a turn, the slide (above left) is a much more common sight for dimmer switches today. Both still work fine, but dimmers are getting smarter.

The dimmer shown above center matches the paddle-style designer switches frequently used in homes today. But it's more than an on/off switch. The little lever to the right is also a slide dimmer switch! It allows you to set the lighting intensity, and each time the switch is turned on by the paddle switch, that's the intensity you get.

Shown at the top right of the page is a variation on this same concept, but it uses a standard toggle-style switch, to fit in with that style, if that's what's in your house.

At right is a variation on the switch/slide design, but the slide is the larger part of the whole, with the push on/off switch tucked nicely below.

And lastly, a switch that's more a touch switch with the dimmer slide a rocker switch on the right. Even more fun, it comes with a remote control. Perfect for watching TV!

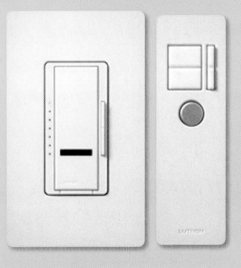

REPLACE AN OUTLET

I REMEMBER WHEN I PURCHASED my first home, at the ripe age of 23. I was quickly faced with outdated everything. My 1950 ranch house, which was the casa de jour in my neighborhood, had those archaic dark brown switches, which made a loud click! The receptacles also matched that lovely color. Since all the trim in the house was going to be painted white, I decided make all the old outlets and switches white as well. And no, I didn't want to paint them either. Can you say wet paint on live outlet = electrical shock! Needless to say, it was a bit time consuming. However, the end result looked great in each room and was well worth it.

Now you may like the color or style of your current outlets, but if you ever need to replace one, here's how you do it.

Replace an Outlet

TIME: 15 minutes

EFFORT LEVEL: Basic

TOOLS AND MATERIALS:
- Screwdrivers—Flat head and Phillips
- Circuit tester
- Wire cutters
- Needle nose pliers
- New receptacle
- Wire nuts

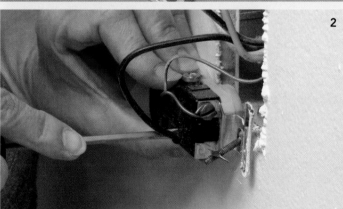

1 Turn off power to the switch (at breaker or fuse box). If you don't have a circuit tester to make sure the power is off, you can plug a radio in and even hear it from the breaker box. Simple. Then start by removing switch plate.

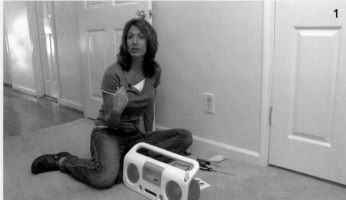

2 With this outlet, the existing wires are stab-style and can be removed by sticking a screwdriver into the corresponding hole next to the wire ...

3 ... then simply pull the wire out of the outlet. Disconnect all the wires and remove the old receptacle.

4 With my new outlet receptacle, I'm using standard screw attachments, so I need to form the wire into a U to best fit around the screw shank. A pair of needle nose pliers works great for this.

5 With your U formed, you may need to tighten or loosen the shape a bit (again, using the needle nose pliers) to get just the right size.

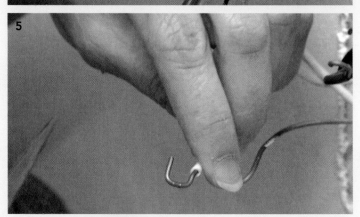

6 When attaching wires, attach the black wire to the copper terminal screw.

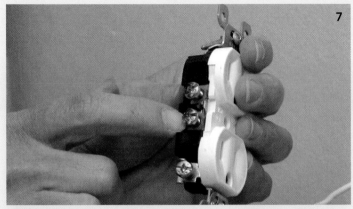

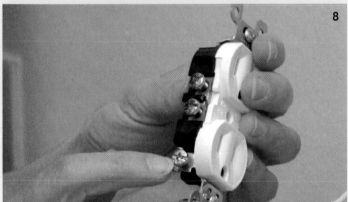

7 The white wire connects to the silver terminal screws ....

8 ...and the green or bare ground wire connects to the green terminal screw. Tighten down the screws until they secure the wiring. Be sure not to over tighten terminal screws as this may cause the wires to pop out from under the terminal screws and break the power connection that feeds the receptacle.

9 Gently push the receptacle back into the wall. Secure it with the long wall screws. Then, turn power back on and test the new outlet

10 Last, but not least, install the new face plate and you're ready to plug the radio back in ... for pleasure, this time!

3 PLUMBING

It's no wonder that your plumbing feels neglected. When things are going great and everything works as expected, you rarely if ever give your plumbing a second thought. Besides, who wants to actually think about how the toilet works or just how all that dirty dishwater makes its way out of your house. It's out of sight, out of mind most of the time ... until there's a problem. And even a running toilet feels like the end of the world if it's 3 A.M. and you can't sleep! Sadly, plumbing problems have a stigma attached to them that a professional plumber is almost always needed and unfortunately plumbers don't run cheap. But the good news is that all is not lost! We're here to tell you that you can dive in and easily take on many plumbing projects and save some cash in the process.

THE FLOW OF A PLUMBING SYSTEM

Your house contains several types of drain systems. You have fixture drains, a soil/vent stack drain, and finally your main drain. Fixture drains are the pipes that drain the wastewater from your sinks and toilets, showers and washing appliances. The soil/vent stack is a large vertical pipe that collects all wastewater from the fixture drains and takes it to the main drain in the basement or underneath the concrete slab of your foundation. This pipe is vented up and through your roof. It has a plug near the base of it so you can unclog or clean it out. The average size house has only one soil/vent stack, but larger homes may have two or more. Finally, there is the main drain. This drainpipe is the largest and slopes to the lowest point under your house. Once it collects the wastewater from the soil stack, it directs the wastewater from your house to either your city sewer drain or your septic tank.

Just like knowing how your electricity comes into your home, knowing how your plumbing routes through your house is the first step in understanding how to take on plumbing projects. While there is no need to create a map for the plumbing system like your electrical circuit map, you do need to know where to turn the water off for the entire house or to a specific location in case there is ever an emergency. If you are using city- or county-provided water, the house's main shut-off valve is located inside the meter box. You will usually find the meter box located near the street. However, my meter box is located halfway down my driveway, 50 yards from the street. Wherever it is, find it now—in an emergency that is the last thing you need to search for.

Plumbers also install a shut-off valve on your main water line as it comes from the meter box into the

house. This is usually found either in your basement or crawl space. From this main water line, smaller lines run throughout your house to feed all the water taps, including one that fills your water heater. Cold water supply lines come directly off the main water line and feed all the cold water taps. Hot water lines tie into the main line coming from your water heater. These water supply lines go directly to the hot water taps throughout your house.

If you are using well water, then you have a pump that forces the water from the well into a main water line that empties into a storage tank inside your house. To stop water flow to the storage tank, simply turn the pump power switch off or turn the shut off valve off on the main water line. When performing repairs on the pump itself, turn off the electrical breaker for the pump at your main electrical panel.

Whichever way the water gets to the house, you will find a shut-off valve on the water supply lines next to your toilets, sinks and washing appliances. Shut-off

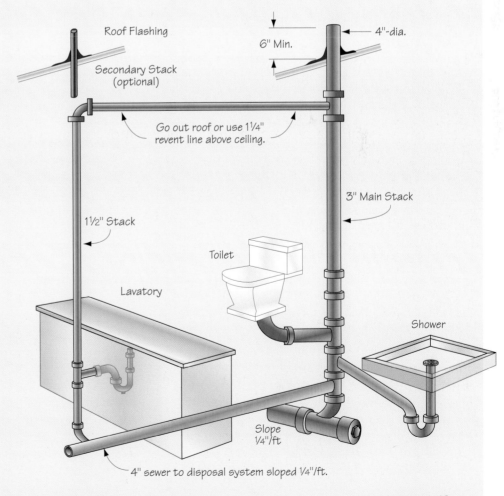

Roof Flashing

Secondary Stack (optional)

6" Min.

4"-dia.

Go out roof or use 1¼" revent line above ceiling.

1½" Stack

3" Main Stack

Toilet

Lavatory

Shower

Slope ¼"/ft

4" sewer to disposal system sloped ¼"/ft.

valves make it easy and convenient to turn the water off at a specific fixture without cutting off water throughout the rest of the house.

As an example for being prepared, Jodi arrived at my house one day finding water pouring out from under my garage doors. Rushing in and advising me of the situation occurring right under my nose, we quickly discovered that the water was seeping through the foundation under the house. Jodi raced up the driveway to turn off the water flow at the meter box. I ran into the basement and turned off the shut off valve on the main water line entering the house from the meter box. Thank goodness the water leak stopped.

Next we had to determine where the leak was on the main water line. Back at the meter box, we turned the water on again. The meter showed continuous water flowing even though we knew it should have stopped at the closed shut off valve at the basement. It didn't. Gallons upon gallons of water kept flowing. This process of elimination proved that the leak was somewhere on the main water line between the meter box and the shut-off valve in the basement.

Fortunately the basement walls and foundation showed no signs of water damage. With shovels in hand, we began digging up the yard next to my house where the flooding appeared to start. Low and behold, there was our leak! There is no telling how much water and money we would have wasted had we not known exactly where our shut off valves were located.

Now that you understand how the water comes into your house, how it goes out, and what you can do to control it, you are prepared to take on some of the more basic plumbing projects.

Starting with your faucets.

FROZEN PIPES

Frozen pipes, while usually a problem in older houses, can occur in any aged home. A few years ago a cold front took hold in Georgia, bitterly cold at that. Waking up, I moseyed down to the kitchen sink to make some coffee. Well, the water trickled, then nothing.

Knowing water tends to expand when it freezes, I quickly went from the moseying state and was fully aware that a pipe was 'frozen', in danger of bursting, or already 'busted'.

I was surprised, as this was a fairly new house and went searching for exposed pipes, leakage, water, or any indication. My first thought was the garage — it was cold and definitely the most exposed part of the house (and least insulated). I went to the bathroom near the garage and checked the tap. No water.

Knowing the water entered the house through the side of the garage, I started sleuthing for the issue. I noticed a reworked patch of sheet rock and on a whim decided to check behind it. Sure enough, there was the copper water pipe, fully exposed. Insulation was on the pipe a few feet above, but nothing where it entered the garage.

I had a strong inkling that this was the issue. I got a hair dryer. Opened all the affected faucets and proceeded to use the hairdryer to slowly thaw the pipe. Note that using a propane torch or other intense heat item may cause the pipe to explode — due to the source heating the pipe too quickly.

So here is the recommended procedure if you isolate the frozen pipe:

• Obtain a slow and mild heating source, like a hair dryer, a heat lamp, mini-heater, etc.

• Open the faucets that are blocked.

• Work the hair dryer's heat from the open faucet toward the frozen area. This approach prevents steam from building and being trapped by the ice—which would cause the pipe to burst.

• The open faucets will clearly indicate when the ice has melted. Whew!

Tips for prevention:

1. Check your pipes to make sure that they are insulated in some manner.

2. Cover the pipe with insulation to retain heat.

3. Note, in extreme cold climates, you can wrap the more exposed pipes with a heating cable. When the temp drops below freezing, plug in that cable.

NOISY PIPES

Once in a while those house pipes may squeak and bang producing a consistently annoying refrain and reminder that it is not going away.

The noise that you hear is usually a pipe or pipes that are too loose or too tight of a fit as they (the pipes) meander through wood framing. This is most commonly associated with hot-water or heating pipes. Most all of us have heard the loud bang when someone shuts off a faucet, which stops the flowing water and then "bang" often appropriately referred to as the "water hammer."

Quiet those Pipes:

Excessive water pressure can cause noisy pipes (apparently in excess of 50 lbs. per sq inch—so how do you figure that out?). You can test for excessive water pressure by securing a pressure gauge to an outdoor faucet. If the pressure is excessive (above 50 lbs psi) install a pressure regulator on your water system.

Get it done:

• Install the pressure regulator.

• Get piping straps or hangers and secure the pipes to the framing.

• If copper pipes are contacting the framing, cut foam pipe insulation to fit past the framing. Remove the straps of hangers if needed. Reinstall the straps or hangers after fitting the insulation.

Muffling the Water Hammer:

Most fixtures and water appliances require air-cushioning chambers. These air chambers simply are short-capped pipe extending up from the water pipe. The dastardly water hammer sound usually occurs due to water that has found its way into the air chamber—where there of course should be air. You need to restore that air.

Let's fix it:

1. Shut off the water main.

2. Open the faucets and drain both hot and cold H$_2$O. Turn the water back on.

3. Close the faucets when you are certain that no air is steadily flowing through the system (no bursts of water / air mixtures).

4. You may have an appliance or plumbing fixture that does not have an air chamber. Drain the lines and install an air chamber on the hot and cold water lines. This is usually done inside the wall behind the appliance or fixture.

5. Remove a short section of pipe that is near the faucet. You will need:

• A T-fitting

• A nipple

• Reducer fitting to attach the following:

• 1 foot length of pipe (that is larger than the supply line). Install a cap fitting.

There you have it, an air chamber. No hammering now needed.

TAKING CARE OF YOUR PLUMBING

Most urbanites or city dwellers have the luxury of having their refuse and waste managed by the municipality that they live in. Sewage refers to not only toilet (black) water, but also bath water, dishwashing, cleaning and laundry (gray) water feed the sewage system. The city's sewer system treats the waste, which thankfully takes that duty out of the homeowner's hands and into theirs. Though we still pay for that welcomed service.

If your home is more rural, or even older, you may have a septic tank that collects the waste that drains from your home. This is essentially an onsite sewage treatment system. As the homeowner you are responsible for taking care of your septic system.

The septic tank separates the solids from the liquid. Bacteria (friendly) decompose the organic solids. The tank then stores the solids until they are removed by pumping. The liquid is delivered to a soil treatment area (known as a drain or leach field) that absorbs the liquid waste.

There are a couple rules of thumb for managing your septic tank. When it needs pumped, call your neighborhood septic person—this part is not a job for the do-it-yourselfer.

1. If you buy a home that has a septic tank you should always make sure that the tank has recently been pumped. Be sure to get verification and proof.

2. The septic tank needs to be pumped out occasionally—depending on usage, size and condition of the septic tank.

a. Most licensed septic "Maintainers" will recommend pumping every 1 to 3 years. They will also evaluate the conditions of the tank and provide you that feedback.

b. Never go more than 36 months between cleanings or evaluations.

3. Additives or cleaners can also be used in your waste system, though their efficacy isn't agreed upon by everyone.

Some enzyme products might have the ability to reduce the amount of oil and grease in the tank. Also, some additives have delivered slight reduction in the amount of effluent solids.

The choice is yours. We happen to use "biological" additives with our septic tank. We try to stay away from the heavy chemical ones.

The key though is don't forget to get the septic pumped or you'll truly be backed up.

REPAIR A FAUCET

DRIP, DRIP, DRIP… YOU'VE HEARD IT BEFORE. THAT incessant dripping cannot be ignored, not to mention it quickly wastes gallons of water. You have two choices, purchase a new faucet or repair the old one. Fixing it yourself is easy enough; in addition you will save some dollars.

Faucets come in four different types; compression, rotating ball, cartridge, and ceramic disc.

By all outward appearances, the ball, cartridge and disk types look nearly the same. Typically found in the kitchen, but making their way into the bathroom, each has a single lever that controls the water flow. Note that the cartridge faucet has some models that are operated with two handles and looks similar to a compression type faucet. The compression type, which is the oldest type of faucet, has two handles. You usually see them in the bathroom. So here's your Jeopardy trivia question: what sets each type apart? Drum roll, please! And the answer is…how they work on the inside. As you can bet, this determines how each is repaired.

Compression Faucet

As the name implies, turning the handles constrict the water flow. With the water turned off, inside each handle a small washer at the base of the compression stem is tightened down to seal off the water flow. Turning the handles on releases the washer from its seat and lets the water run. Unfortunately, compression type faucets are notorious for leaks because these small washers wear out over time and can no longer completely seal off the water. Replacing the washer, rubber O-ring or removing the corrosion from the valve seat usually does the trick.

Rotating Ball Faucet

Again, as the name implies, there is either a plastic or metal ball inside the faucet base. The single lever rotates over this ball, which has several openings to allow water flow. One opening aligns to the spout. By shifting the lever back and forth, you control how much water gets through that opening. The other openings on the ball align to the hot and cold water supply lines. Shifting the lever side to side controls the hot or cold temperature.

And you guessed it, shifting the lever again and again wears down the inside components and they need replacing. Fortunately there are repair kits that include everything you need, just know your model number to match it up to the right kit.

Cartridge Faucet

Nothing like calling a spade a spade, with this type of faucet, they couldn't get any clearer on naming this type of faucet. Inside this faucet body is a cartridge that lifts up and down to operate the water flow. On the cartridge are several O-rings that are used to seal the openings for the spout and the hot and cold water supply. As you lift the lever up, (or as with the two-handle model, turn the knob) the O-rings clear the opening for the water to come out of the spout. The higher you raise the lever, the more powerful the flow. Moving it side to side releases the O-rings, which allows the hot and cold water to flow and allows you to adjust the temperature (just like in the rotating ball type). But alas, those O-rings or the cartridge itself can wear out over time causing that annoying drip. Replacing the O-rings or the entire cartridge is simple enough. The best part is everything you usually need comes in a kit. Again, match your faucet model number with the kit for the right parts.

Ceramic Disc Faucets

This is our favorite type of faucet. Why, you ask? Well folks, they're basically maintenance free. These bad boys are the new kids on the block when it comes to faucet types. Hailing from the latest in European design, they look very similar to the rotating ball and cartridge type faucets. However inside the base of these faucets are two kiln-fired ceramic disks that slide over each other, sort of like a sliding glass door lying on its side, to allow the water to flow. When the water flow is off, the disks create a virtually indestructible seal between them that no water can squeak through.

On the offbeat chance your disk faucet is leaking, then I guess you are going to have to move. Or you can purchase a ceramic disk repair kit and replace it in no time. Don't forget that faucet model number when you go to get your kit. Be sure to check those inlet holes as well, sometimes they get clogged or corroded.

Now, let's fix those drips!

Repair a Faucet

TIME: About one hour

EFFORT LEVEL: Basic

TOOLS AND MATERIALS:

- Replacement cartridge kit for your faucet
- Phillips head screwdrive
- Adjustable wrench
- Needle nose pliers
- Utility knife
- Plumber's grease

Only basic tools are needed to work on this plumbing project. You'll need a pair of tongue-and-groove pliers, a couple of screwdrivers and some needle nose pliers.

1 Cut the water to the sink at the shut-off valve.

2 After you have shut the water off to the faucet you will need to "bleed the line" of the water. Position the handle to the "on" position to drain the remaining water.

3 At first the water will be strong since the water has been under pressure inside the water lines. But quickly it will become a trickle. Remember to turn the handle back to the off position. Cover the drain hole to prevent losing any parts.

4 With a flathead screwdriver, gently pry up the decorative cap on the handle that conceals the handle screw. Be careful not to scratch your handle's finish.

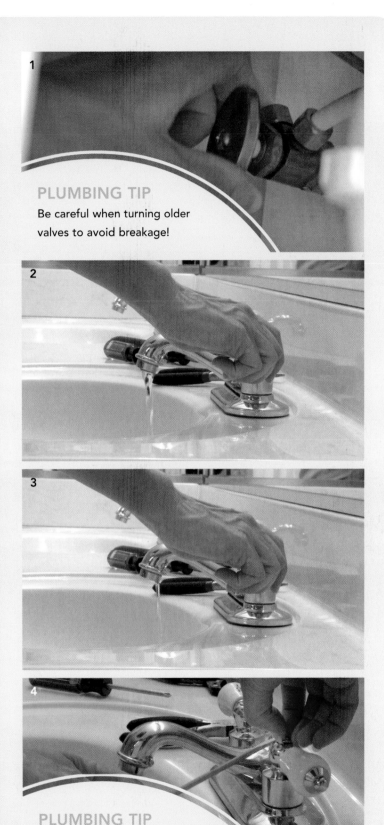

PLUMBING TIP
Be careful when turning older valves to avoid breakage!

PLUMBING TIP
A washcloth over the sink drain will keep small parts from disappearing!

5 With your screwdriver, remove the handle screw. Sometimes you may run into rust making it hard to get this screw out. Use a bit of rust remover to make it easier.

6 Gently lift the handle off the faucet base to expose the cartridge assembly.

7 In our case, we have a pretty typical faucet type for the bathroom, a compression style faucet. So we will need to purchase the exact replacement cartridge for our faucet.

8 With a pair of tongue and groove pliers or an adjustable wrench, remove the locking nut that secures the cartridge to the faucet base.

9 With the locking nut removed, the cartridge is exposed. Pay particular attention to the plastic tab and how it fits into the brass fitting. The new cartridge needs to fit the same way.

10 With a pair of needle nose pliers, oh so gently pull the cartridge stem straight up to dislodge it from the base. You may have to gently use your adjustable wrench to help pry it free. Again, take a look at how it comes out and how the pieces are situated together at the bottom of the cartridge.

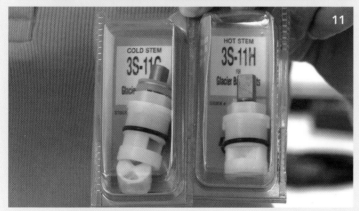

11 Here are our replacement cartridges. Notice that they look identical except that on the package one is marked "C" for the cold water handle and the other is marked "H" for the hot. It's very important that you get the right cartridge for the right handle.

12 Place the cartridge in the handle base and push it down into place. There may be some water in the hole where the cartridge goes. That's fine, you can soak it up with a cloth.

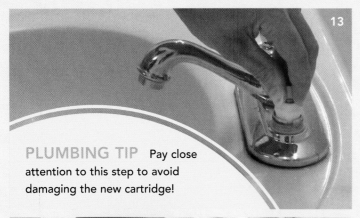

PLUMBING TIP Pay close attention to this step to avoid damaging the new cartridge!

13 Be careful not to force your new stem into place. It should be seated perfectly straight and completely in the hole.

14 Take the locking nut that secures the cartridge to the base and twist it into place.

15 Tighten it all up with your pair of pliers or your wrench. Don't over-tighten it as this may damage the new cartridge.

16 Take your handle and slide it back down over the cartridge stem. Your cartridge should be on in the "off" position, so be sure your handle is in the "off" position as well.

17 Tighten back down the screw that secures the handle to the faucet base, but don't over-tighten it as it may crack the new stem.

18 Put the decorative cap back over the screw opening and press it into place.

19 Turn the water back on from underneath your sink at the shut-off valve and then test your new cartridge for drips. If the water comes on when the handle is in the "off" position and stops when the handle is in the "on" position, then your cartridge is installed incorrectly. Shut the water off, disassemble the handle and give the new cartridge a half turn. Reinstall the handle, turn back on the water and test again. That should correct the problem.

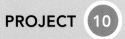

INSTALL A NEW FAUCET

FAUCET REPAIR IS A QUICK AND AFFORDABLE WAY to keep the water flowing. But sometimes your faucet may need more than a repair; it may need to be replaced. With so many styles and finishes to choose from now, replacing your faucet is also a nice way to help upgrade the look and functionality of your sink. If you are replacing your faucet, but not your sink, you may need to purchase a faucet that requires the same number of holes in the sink as your old one. However, most single-hole faucets can be used on a three-hole cutout due to the deck plate that comes with it to hide those unnecessary holes.

To remove the old faucet, shut off the water to the sink and turn the faucet on to drain the water lines. Disconnect the water supply lines and remove the locking nuts that hold the faucet to the sink, then lift the old faucet out. Disconnect the drain pipe and remove the locking nut that holds the drain flange in place. Install the new flange according to your manufacturer's instructions. Now you are ready to put that new faucet in place!

Install a New Faucet

TIME: 1 hour

EFFORT LEVEL: Basic

TOOLS AND MATERIALS:
- New faucet
- Adjustable wrench
- Basin wrench (for tight spaces under cabinet)
- Plumber's putty
- New water supply lines (if necessary)

1. On the clean surface of your sink, align the rubber gasket over the holes in the sink. If your model doesn't come with this separate gasket, then the gasket may be a part of the faucet itself.

2. Place your new faucet over the gasket and seat it into place. Or if you have made a putty seal, gently set the faucet in place and press it firmly into the putty.

3 Underneath the sink you should be able to see the handle shanks and the lift rod for the sink stopper.

4 Thread the mounting nuts that come with your faucet onto the handle shanks and hand tighten them. As you do tighten the nuts down it will cause the putty, if you used it under the faucet, to ooze out. That is necessary to make a sealed edge. You can use your fingernail to scrape the excess away.

5 Attach the existing water supply lines to each handle shank. Be sure the hot water supply line attaches to the left handle shank and the cold water supply line attaches to the right handle shank.

6 Using an adjustable wrench, tighten down the nuts on each supply line, but be careful not to over-tighten them as it will damage the lines.

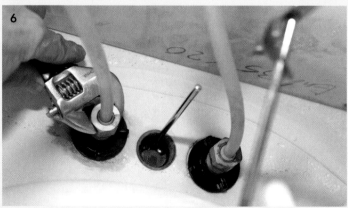

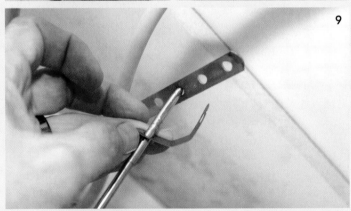

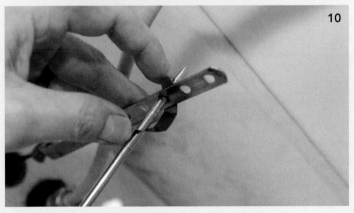

7 To install the parts necessary to use the sink stopper, first take the metal strap called a link and slide it onto the lift rod that's between the two handle shanks. Use the thumbscrew to tighten the lift rod to the link.

8 Attach the rod with the plastic seal ball on the end to the drain body. Use the rod nut to secure it to the drain.

9 The height of the rod coming from the drain may vary. That is why the link has many holes so you can help align the two perfectly.

10 Align the link to the rod coming from the drain body. Make sure the rod is pressed all the way down before deciding which hole to use on the link. Use the spring clip to secure the rod to the link. Pull the lift rod on top of the faucet to test the stopper.

INSTALL AN ICE MAKER
SHUT-OFF VALVE

MANY OLDER HOMES SIMPLY DO NOT HAVE a shut-off valve for the ice maker line near their refrigerator. Most times the valve is located somewhere along the water line in their basement or crawl space. Ours used to be located right near the water heater. That wasn't too convenient. We recently purchased a new refrigerator and the delivery and installation were free, with one condition: the shut-off valve had to be reachable while installing the new fridge. or they wouldn't make the connection for us. Steve didn't want to lug the huge refrigerator around once they brought it, so we decided installing a shut-off valve was a small price to pay to have them hook up our new appliance. We thought since we had to do it, it would be a good project to show you how to do it.

Ice Maker Valve

TIME: 45 minutes

EFFORT LEVEL: Basic

TOOLS AND MATERIALS:
- Shut-off valve kit
- Pipe cutter
- Teflong tape, or plumber's putty
- Wrench, or pliers

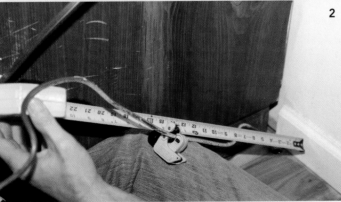

1   Out at your water meter or where the water line comes into your house, shut off the water and drain the line by turning on a faucet until the line is empty. Then, pull out your old refrigerator to expose the water line for the ice maker. I let Steve do it, so get some help if yours is too heavy to move.

2   With a tape measure, measure up the water line about two feet. We decided this is where we want the shut-off valve because it would be easier to reach than having to bend down way behind the refrigerator if we ever needed to quickly turn it off.

3 We had to cut the copper water line. To make the cut:

A. Slightly tighten the pipe cutter. Do not force it—you do not want to crimp the tubing.

B. Complete one revolution.

C. Slightly tighten the cutter again.

D. Complete another revolution.

E. Continue this process until the tubing splits in half.

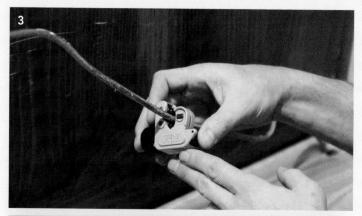

4 Now there was a bit of water still trapped in our water line, so have a bucket handy to catch any of the spill in case yours does too.

5 Place the nut from the valve assembly kit onto the tubing with the open threads facing the cut end of the tubing. Place the compression sleeve on the tubing, in front of the nut. Once the nut is tightened, it will make the connection water-tight.

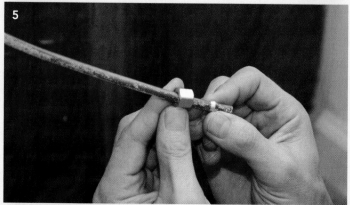

6 Wrap both ends of the valve assembly's threads with Teflon tape. You could use plumber's putty to coat the threads, but I think it's messy and could actually block the water flow if you use too much.

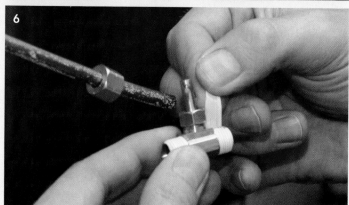

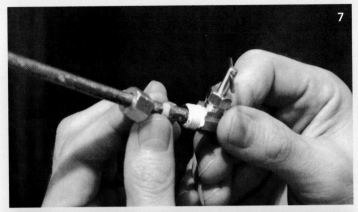

7 Insert the end of the tubing into one end of the valve assembly. Hand tighten the nut. Pay attention to the tubing, so that it is firmly against the valve assembly and does not slide out.

8 Make sure that the turn knob on the valve assembly is in the off position as you are attaching it to the tubing. The knob is perpendicular to the water line. When you turn the water back on, it will readily show you if there are any leaks at these pressure points.

9 Next, grab two wrenches. Use one wrench on the nut, the other wrench on the valve assembly to securely hold the assembly while tightening. Do the same thing with the other nut starting at step 3. Again, do not over-tighten. Also check if the nut securing the handle stem is tight. The first time I installed the valve assembly it was loose and water shot everywhere.

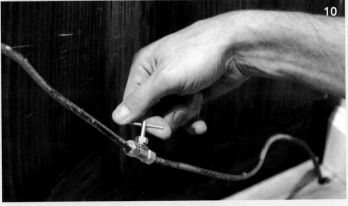

10 Turn the water back on either at your meter or just inside the house. Now check for leaks at the valve. If all is good to go, open up the valve to allow the water to flow to your refrigerator. Voila! Another job well done!

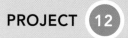
INSTALL A KITCHEN SINK

WHETHER YOU ARE INSTALLING OR REPLACING the kitchen sink, these steps are the same with the exception of removing the old one first. If you are installing a new sink and the hole in the counter top has not been cut, make sure that you use the template that comes with your sink to make that cut precise (follow manufacturers' directions). Instructions for cutting the template should be on the template itself. Remember, measure twice, cut once!

For our application, we are replacing our old sink with a new one. The difference here is that our old one had two basins. Our new one is a big basin sink with only one drain. Therefore, we had to plan to relocate our garbage disposal to the middle of our cabinet base and that meant getting new plumbing drain pipes to accommodate this change. Also, we replaced our old disposal with a newer, more powerful model (page 95). Here's how you installed just the sink.

Install a Kitchen Sink

TIME: About one hour

EFFORT LEVEL: Basic, or intermediate if cutting countertop

TOOLS AND MATERIALS:
- Wrench
- Screwdriver
- Caulk and caulk gun
- Power drill with hole saw
- Putty knife

If new installation;
- All tools above
- Jigsaw

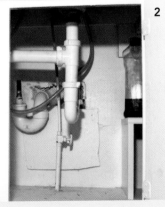

1 Our old sink wasn't *that* bad, but we definitely wanted to upgrade the look. The stainless steel was very much in keeping with our overall style of the kitchen, but I didn't like the fact that I couldn't get big pots or pans in the sink to wash them easily. So this bad boy had to go!

2 When replacing your sink, inspect your plumbing. Like we mentioned, we were trading our two drains in for one. If that is your case, study the current configuration so you can plan how much pipe you will need to accommodate your new sink.

3 To remove the old sink, first turn off the water at the shut-off valves, hopefully located under your sink.

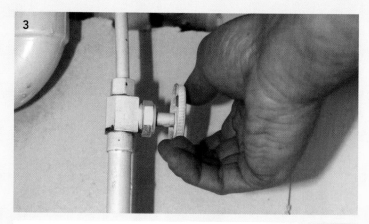

4 Next, turn on the faucet to drain any excess water from the lines, and disconnect the supply lines from the faucet. You might need to have a bucket on stand-by if there is any water still in the lines.

5 Disconnect the drain pipe from the sink and if you do have a garbage disposal like us, you will need to disconnect that, too. That bucket will be price-less when getting rid of that drain pipe.

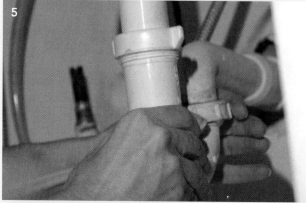

6 Underneath the sink, loosen the clips that se-cure the sink to the cabinet. Some are screws that will need to be removed and some are clamps that you turn by hand. You will also have silicone sealant around the top edge of the sink where it rests on the coun-tertop. Use a putty knife to help pry the sink away.

7 Gently lift the old sink out of the cabinet. This sink was pretty light; however, some sinks are cast iron and are super heavy. Have someone on stand-by if you need help lifting yours out. Remove the old faucet if you are reinstalling it on your new sink.

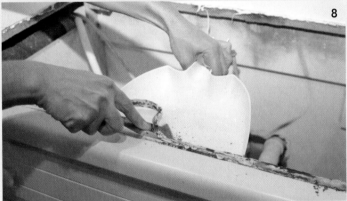

8 Now the gross part! Using a putty knife or a 5-in-1 tool, carefully scrape away all the old sealant from around the edges of the sink. You can also use a mild detergent to get up any stains. If you do use a detergent, rinse the area so the sealant you will be applying with adhere to the surface.

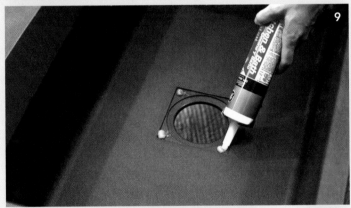

9 Now you need to attach the drain flange to your new sink. It's a good idea to rest your sink between two chairs so you have it elevated and can work from underneath it with ease. Using a silicone sealant, apply it around the indention for the flange.

10 Carefully place the sink flange down into the sealant. Press the edges firmly. This will cause the excess sealant to ooze out from under the flange.

11 With a clean, lint-free cloth, wipe up all the excess sealant. You may have to use a tiny bit of mineral spirits to clean up the sealant.

12 Take your plumber's putty and roll out a thin rope of sealer. Place this around the bottom of your drain ring. Our ring goes to the new garbage disposal we will be installing with our new sink. Some sinks come with a drain strainer and some don't. You may need to purchase yours separately.

13 Firmly press the drain ring in place and wipe away the excess putty that is squeezed out.

14 We then attached the garbage disposal mounting ring underneath the sink and tightened it down on the drain ring. This is what the garbage disposal will attach to once it mounted.

15 We decided that since we were installing a new faucet we would attach it while we had the sink still out. We followed the manufacturer's instructions to mount the faucet.

16 Then we attached the water supply lines, again while the sink was still uninstalled because it makes it a whole lot easier to tighten all the mounting nuts before the sink is in place.

17 Using a caulk gun and the tube of silicone sealant, run a bead of sealant around the perimeter of the sink opening. Some say to run the bead of sealant under the sink lip. Either way is fine.

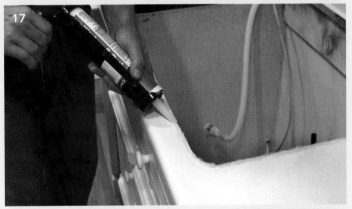

18 With the clips attached to the sides of the sink, gently set the sink into place. We always start at the back first and then drop the front into place. You can better control the sink as you are seating it into the sealant.

19 Once you have your sink in place, reconnect your water supply lines at your faucet and shut-off valve. If you have a garbage disposal, reconnect it.

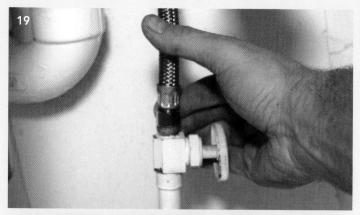

20 Also, reconnect your drain pipe to the drain pipe body attached to your sink. If you have a garbage disposal, reconnect the pipe to it.

21 This is a far cry from the sink we had just an hour ago! Now I can get Steve to wash all those big pots and pans I like to dirty up when cooking!!!

SINK TIPS   Whether you are installing a new faucet or reinstalling the old one, it is best to install it when the sink is out and resting upside down on a towel to prevent scratches. It is so much easier to make all the necessary connections while it is out than when it is in the cabinet and you are working on your back in that tiny space.

Also, install the drain flange while the sink is out. We propped ours up between two chair seats so we could have easy access underneath the sink to set the drain properly.

Some directions say to apply the caulk underneath the sink rim before setting it in place. I have done that and I have applied directly to the countertop and then set the sink in place. Either is fine.

REPLACE A GARBAGE DISPOSAL

WE DECIDED IT WAS TIME TO UPGRADE OUR garbage disposal when we replaced our old kitchen sink. You don't have to upgrade anything when you replace a sink...you can always reinstall your current garbage disposal and reinstall your faucet, too. But I insisted after our last big family dinner that it was time to give our clean up an extra boost, so Steve dipped into his piggybank and granted me my wish with a new disposal...he also surprised me with a new faucet to go with all our fancy new stuff … I was overjoyed!

If you don't have an existing garbage disposal we recommend you hire a licensed electrician to run power for your disposal switch. Then you are ready to install your disposal. Steve and I always recommend that you read all the instructions that come with your disposal. Installation is pretty straight forward, but some manufacturers may have a special instruction with their models.

PLUMBING

Garbage Disposal

TIME: About one hour

EFFORT LEVEL: Basic to intermediate

TOOLS AND MATERIALS:
- Wrench
- Screwdriver
- Wire nuts
- Wire cutters or wire strippers
- Plumber's Putty

INSTALLATION TIPS: If there's any shaking or rattling going on, tighten down the screws on the mounting ring. Also, remember there is a power reset button on the bottom of your disposal in the event the power goes out or the breaker gets tripped. Once power is restored and your disposal won't start, hit the reset and all should be well.

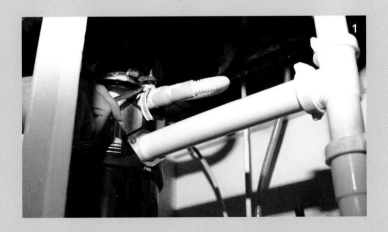

1 The first thing you have to do was get that old garbage disposal out of there! So, shut off the breaker at the breaker box so there is no electrical power to the switch. Then disconnect the drain pipe from the dishwasher if yours is connected. Ours was attached with a clamp, so we had to unscrew that.

2 You will also have to disconnect the drain pipe from the side as well. Use your screwdriver to remove those screws.

3 Disconnect the power to the old disposal. We decided that we had enough cable where we could just cut the wire and still have enough to reach our new disposal location.

4 While holding the disposal, take a screwdriver or the "wrenchette" that comes with your new disposal to turn and release the disposal body from the mounting ring.

5 After removing the old disposal, inspect the existing sink flange and mounting ring from your old disposal. If you can reuse these for your new disposal, you can jump down to step #13. If you need to install the sink flange and mounting ring, go to the next step.

6 Remove the old mounting ring and pry off the old sink flange. Take plumber's putty and roll a thick rope and wrap it around the new sink flange.

7 Gently place the new sink flange in the bottom of the sink and firmly press down. Some of the putty will ooze out on the sides, but this is normal and good because it ensures that you are getting a tight seal. Just wipe the excess away with a cloth.

8 Our manufacturer recommending that we weigh the flange down with a heavy weight such as the garbage disposal placed on a towel to protect the sink from scratches.

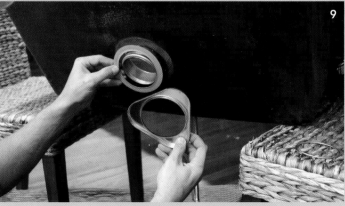

9 From underneath the sink, slide the fiber gasket onto the sink flange.

10 Then slide the flat, triangle shaped ring onto the fiber gasket.

11 Slide the mounting ring with the three tightening screws over the flat ring and push it flush to the bottom of the sink.

12 Attach the snap ring under the mounting ring to help hold it place. You could use an extra rubber band to help hold it in place, too.

13 With your screwdriver, tighten down the three screws that secure the mounting ring to the sink making sure that all of the pieces are flush and correctly seated together.

14 If you are connecting your dishwasher line to your disposal: Lay the disposal on its side and with a screwdriver, knock out the plastic tab on the intake valve. Be sure to remove the plastic tab from inside the disposal chamber.

15 On the bottom of the disposal, unscrew the electrical cover plate, leaving the cardboard shield in place. Pull out the wires and attach the cable connector to the bottom of the disposal.

16 Run the electrical wiring through the cable connector on the bottom of the disposal and out through the opening of the cover plate.

17 Tighten the cable connector to secure the wire to the base of the disposal and spread out the three wires of the cable. You may need to cut away some of the sheathing to expose the raw wires.

18 First attach the ground wire to the green, ground screw with your screwdriver. Then using a wire nut, join the two white wires together, twisting the wire nuts clock-wise. Then joint the two black wires together using a wire nut.

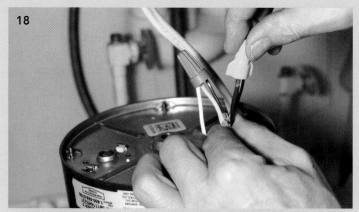

19 Gently tuck all the wires back into the wire opening and attach the cover plate with the screw provided.

20 Gently lift the disposal body into place on the mounting ring and twist it into place. Make sure it clicks into place and is firmly seated or it will start to rattle the first time you turn it on.

21 If you are draining your dishwasher through your disposal you will need to reconnect the drain line that feeds from the dishwasher to the intake valve located at the top of the disposal. We used a wire clamp to hold ours in place.

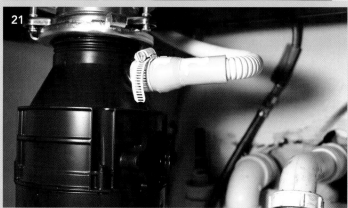

UNCLOG A DRAIN

BLOCKAGE CAN OCCUR IN ANY OF THE drain types coursing through your house: in the fixture drains, or maybe the soil stack, or possibly at the main drain. The key to troubleshooting a clog is to figure out if only one fixture is affected, or more. Don't flush the toilet, as it may overflow and create a mess.

Go check the drains of either the kitchen or another bathroom. If two or more fixtures are plugged and won't clear it is indicative of something lodged down the line in a main drain. If no drains work, it's time to call a plumber. They will probably start at the soil stack and see if they can flush out the problem at the soil stack plug. This is quite messy and definitely worth the service to have them do it.

Probably the most common blockage occurs in a trap at the sink or where a pipe makes a turn. Let's first take a look at unplugging a clogged sink and then the steps in removing a P-trap.

If the plunger "plunging" fails, remove the P-trap. The P-trap is the u-shaped section of pipe located under the sink. You will find P-traps under tubs and sinks.

Sooner or later, due to wear and tear, or that sinking feeling of a ring or earring falling down the drain, you'll need to take apart a trap.

Trap pipes fit together with slip-joint connections. These types of connections let you twist and turn the components so that they align correctly. You secure the assembly with the slip nuts.

PLUMBING

Unclog a Drain

TIME: 10 minutes to 1 hour

EFFORT LEVEL: Basic

TOOLS AND MATERIALS:
- Wrench (if metal drain connections)
- Rubber gloves
- Sink plunger
- Petroleum jelly
- Towel
- Bucket
- Wire hanger
- If needed: Slip-joint pliers, replacement washers and slip nuts, plumber's tape

TIPS:
- What about the chemical liquid clog dissolvers? These can be handy, however many experts suggest that using these chemicals is tough on the pipes, not to mention the environmental concerns that these create downstream. We recommend that you try to remove the clog with the above steps first. If you have to resort to a chemical, use it once. If that doesn't work, call the plumber.
- We recommend keeping two plungers around, a sink plunger and toilet plunger. Use these separately with their respective fixtures and function

1 First, try to use a sink plunger to get that clog out of there. You will need to remove the drain stopper if your sink has one. Use a cloth to plug the overflow vent—this helps increase the plunger's suction.

2 A little trick you can also do to get better suction is to apply petroleum jelly to the rim of the plunger. This will seal up any uneven gaps around the plunger once you place it over the drain opening.

TIP Use petroleum jelly to ensure proper plunger seal.

3 If this doesn't work, it's time to get out the gloves and get down to business. Time to pull out the old trusty coat hanger. This is a great tool for cleaning out the P-trap of the drain pipe.

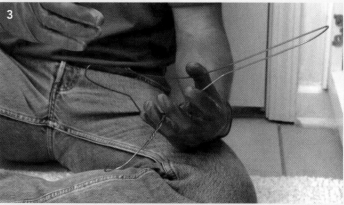

4 Or if the clog is not found immediately in the drain pipe under the sink, then using a sink auger will hopefully hit the clog in the pipes behind the wall and push it on through.

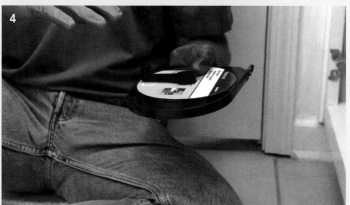

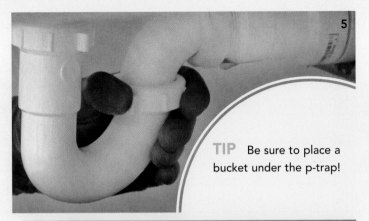

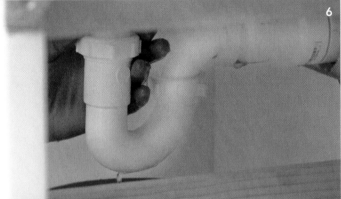

TIP Be sure to place a bucket under the p-trap!

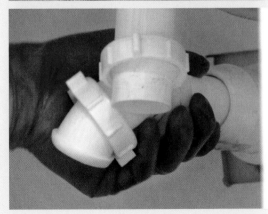

5 Starting at the P-trap, loosen the washer and nut securing the pipes together. You may need to use an adjustable wrench to loosen them.

6 Now water is going to drain out as you loosen it, so have a bucket underneath the pipe to catch all the dirty water.

7 Using the coat hanger, push it through the bend in the P-trap where the clog could have formed. Trust me, you want to do this over that bucket!

8 If the clog isn't in the P-trap, then disconnect the drain pipe that is feeding into the wall. Again, you may have to use a wrench to loosen this connections.

9 Stretch out some of the sink auger cable. About 2 to 3 feet to start with.

10 At the drain opening, gently but firmly push the cable into the drain. You'll begin to feel the cable turn, but just keep feeding it into the drain until you feel it hit something. If it does, then push the cable back and forth, feeding more cable into the drain until you feel it release and it can be pushed without resistance. Gently reel the cable back in. You will either push the clog through or pull the clog out on the end of your auger cable. If the clog is still there, it is further down the line than you can reach and unfortunately it is time to call the plumber.

11 When Steve was putting the drain pipe back together, he noticed the nut was broken. It's a great idea to inspect your drain pipes just to make sure they are all in good shape and won't cause you problems down the road.

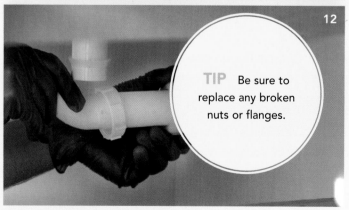

TIP Be sure to replace any broken nuts or flanges.

12 To reconnect the pipes, make sure they align and that you slide the smaller, plastic washer in place before you tighten the plastic nut.

13 If you use a wrench, just make sure you don't over tighten the nut because this could cause your nut to snap and break. Then you'll have a leaky pipe to fix!

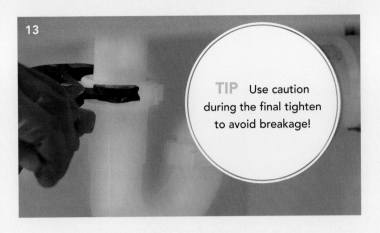

TIP Use caution during the final tighten to avoid breakage!

CLOGGED TUB DRAIN   A clogged tub drain can be frustrating to say the least. Standing in your shower water is no fun and cleaning it out can be daunting if you don't have access to the drain pipe underneath. Our best advice for tub clogs is to stat out with the plunger to see if you can dislodge it. If that doesn't work, remove the tub stopper very carefully. Sometimes just a collection of hair right at the bend can be pulled up when the stopper is removed. Using a sink snake is also an option. If all this fails, you might want to try removing the screws to the stopper lever in your tub. Remove the cover and take off the screws that hold the stopper plunger. Gently pull the plunger up and you might be really surprised how much hair and stuff is trapped there. If you do this, though, make sure you study how it is positioned as you are taking it out to make sure you reinstall it the correct way.

CLOGGED TOILET TIP   *Jodi:* When my daughter turned 2 years old, she took an interest in our hall bathroom toilet and we started potty training her right away. We did all the things the books recommended to build her confidence and make her potty time stress free. We were so amazed that she grasped the whole experience pretty quickly. As the months of practice worn on, she began to take care of business herself without "worrying" mom and dad about her need to go…she was very independent. That's when our plumbing woes began. Poor thing, she understood just about everything when it came to the toilet and what she was supposed to do, except one thing: how much toilet paper to use. She loved toilet paper. Handfuls upon handfuls would make their way into the bowl and only about half got safely through the drain. In no time, I became the world champ on unclogging that toilet, no matter what Hannah threw at it. And while a plunger that fits tightly around the opening can work its charms, nothing, I mean nothing, could withstand the toilet auger! Now that's a tool that's worth its weight in gold and can save you a visit from the trusty plumber. My only advice is that I first bought the cheapest one that didn't have a rubber guard around the coils to protect the bottom of toilet bowl from scratches. The second one I purchased did and I was glad since I had remodeled the house and put in all new toilets.

Toilets

Sad to say, but when I was a young girl, mom or dad were always yelling, "Jiggle the handle, the toilet's running!" Somehow that saying stuck, but it wasn't funny to my friends when we'd prank call people late at night and I'd ask (too quickly), "Is your toilet running…oh, did I say that? I meant refrigerator". I'd hang my head in shame. Having a running toilet is as annoying as those childish pranks, and you can end the misery by just a few tweaks to your toilet.

My parents were spot on; jiggling the handle sometimes stops the toilet from running. However, that generally is a stopgap measure. What it really means is that your lift chain needs adjusting on the handle arm inside your tank. Moving it one or two holes higher on the arm usually does the trick. If all the jiggling in the world still doesn't stop your toilet from running, then it's on to PLAN B (page 111). Here are some steps below that might remedy the problem. Don't rule out that your tank assembly may need replacing. If so, it's no big deal. Tank assemblies typically come in kits. Rest assured the tank water you are about to put your hand in is clean,

even if yours is brown…that just means you have rust in the bottom of the tank.

Many times, the tank's water level is simply too high and spilling into the overflow tube—causing the toilet to consistently run. A good rule of thumb is to keep the water approximately a ½ inch from the top of the overflow pipe.

FLOAT ARM FLUSHING MODEL

There are two ways to adjust the tank's water level by lowering the float ball. You can tighten the small screw on

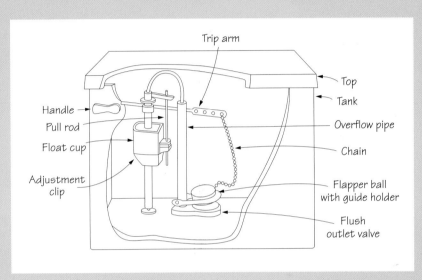

top of the ball cock with a screwdriver. Alternatively, you can grab and gently bend the metal arm connected to the float ball so that it's a tad lower than before. Flush the toilet to monitor the new level and readjust as needed.

FLOAT CUP FLUSHING MODEL

On the float cup model you will see a metal clip that slides up and down. Sliding the clip up raises the water level. Sliding it down lowers the water level. Adjust the float cup to the appropriate height and test the toilet by flushing.

HOW TO ADJUST A TOILET FLAPPER

If the above steps fail, it's time to examine the flapper and remedy the situation. Look around the flapper and bowl and try to notice if there is anything you can adjust to correct the problem:

- Is the chain catching on anything?
- What about the flapper—is it catching on the chain? Is it catching on its hinge?

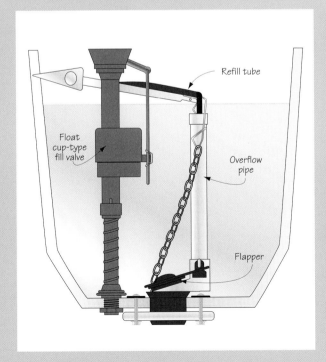

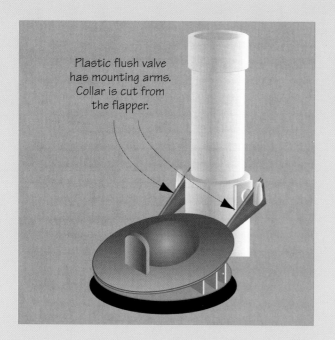

Plastic flush valve has mounting arms. Collar is cut from the flapper.

Unbalanced Toilet

Nothing could spell possible disaster like a toilet that shifts back and forth when you take a seat. While the kids may think it's like a rollercoaster, we all know that a moving toilet is a bad thing…a very bad thing. Fortunately, there are few trouble shooting things you can do make that porcelain throne stable again.

First off, check to make sure the anchor bolts on either side of the toilet base are securely tightened. Just pop off the decorative cap and with your adjustable wrench tighten those babies down. If that doesn't work, it's time to go to back to the drawing board.

• Is the flapper aligning and sealing with the flush valve seat? If not, realign it and your problem may be resolved.

• Is the flapper simply just old, cracked or stiff?

If the above observations and corrections don't fix the problem, replace the flapper.

How to Replace a Toilet Flapper

1. With the water turned off, the lid removed, and as much water flushed out as possible, use a sponge to absorb the rest of the water.

2. Remove the chain from flush lever arm

3. Take off the old flapper and replace it with a new one that comes with a lift chain and collar.

4. Place the new flapper's collar on the overflow pipe and slide it down.

5. Attach the chain to the trip lever by hooking it into one of the holes—have a little slack in the chain so the flapper sits flush on the opening. The right length of chain allows the flapper to open when you push the handle and close all of the way when the tank is emptied.

6. You're ready for testing. Turn on the shut-off valve so the tank fills with water. Flush the toilet and adjust the chain and trip lever if needed.

Hopefully that fixes the problem, if not, you will need to replace the toilet fill valve with a new one.

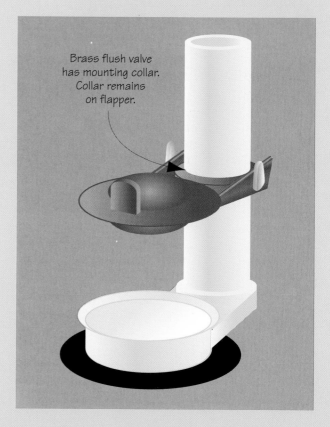

Brass flush valve has mounting collar. Collar remains on flapper.

DRAWING BOARD – here's a neat little trick I learned from Cory, a Master Plumber friend of mine. With a putty knife or 5-in-1 tool, remove the caulk around the base of the toilet. Then using one at a time, stack pennies under the edge of the toilet that has the gap, usually you'll need only one or two at the most. You can also use a Popsicle stick as a wedge, but make sure that whatever you use is under the edge and not poking out. Run a fresh bead of silicone caulk around the toilet base and you are good to go.

Replacing a Toilet Wax Ring

If your toilet has been unbalanced and rocking back and forth for some time now, there's a good chance the wax ring has pulled away from its seal and water could be leaking from the base of the toilet. If this has happened, then the simple solution is to replace the wax ring.

Start by turning off the water at the shut-off valve, flush the toilet, and remove the water from the tank and bowl. Then remove the water supply line from the back side of the toilet. Loosen the anchor bolts that secure the toilet to the floor and lift up the toilet. You will see your old wax ring, half of which will be stuck to the drain flange on the floor and probably half will still be attached to the bottom of the toilet. With a putty knife, scrape off the old wax on the floor and on the toilet. Wipe both clean.

Now there are two schools of thought on where to attach the new wax ring. Some say to attach the wax ring to the bottom of the toilet. Some say to place the wax ring on the drain flange. Personally, I have found that it is easiest to place the ring on the bottom of the toilet and then set it into place. Once I lift that heavy toilet I have a hard time lining the toilet up with the floor ring mainly because I can't see it. And remember, wax rings are very persnickety. You can't get a second chance to lift it back up and try again…what's the saying, "a card laid is a card played"? Well, wax rings are no different. So slap that puppy on the bottom and set the toilet firmly into place on the anchor bolts. Go ahead and sit on the toilet just make sure there is a tight seal with the wax ring and then tighten the bolts down. Put on the decorative caps and you are back in business.

Replacing a Toilet

If you read the section above, replacing or installing a new toilet is pretty much spelled out with replacing a wax ring. The only other steps involved are assembling the toilet (if it's a two-piece toilet according to the manufacturer's directions) and installing the drain flange on the floor at the drain opening. Align the anchor bolts straight across from each other on the flange so they will line up with the holes in the toilet base. Most will have plastic clips to help hold them in place and keep them straight up. Attach the wax ring to the bottom of the toilet and set into place. Tighten down the bolts, attach the water supply line to the back side of the toilet, and turn on the water to fill the tank. Most toilet tanks have the fill valve already installed, but if not, jump over to our fill valve section to read how to do that. Caulk around the base of the toilet with silicone caulking and you are done.

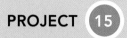
REPLACE A TOILET FILL VALVE

OKAY, SO YOU ARE AT PLAN B. Honestly, replacing a fill valve is no biggie. Of course, you can make a big deal and brag to your friends how you saved the day by laboring and sweating to fix that darn toilet…we won't tell.

Fill valve replacement kits are fairly standard. Pick up a quality kit from your favorite hardware store. Familiarize yourself with the unit and read the instructions that come with it.

Replace a Toilet Fill Valve

TIME: 1½ hours

EFFORT LEVEL: Basic to intermediate

TOOLS AND MATERIALS:
- New fill valve kit
- Wrench or adjustable pliers
- Screwdriver
- Sponge
- Bucket

INSTALLATION TIPS:
- If the water level in your tank is too low, it will prevent the bowl from adequately flushing.
- The coupling nut is not put on using the old "righty-tighty" adage. Remember it goes on counter-clockwise.

TIP Be gentle with older valves—they can become brittle and break!

TIP Follow all manufacturer's instructions.

1 Shut off the water at the toilet's shut-off valve. Now if your valve is old or corroded, you might have to use a pair of pliers to turn it. Using a little WD-40 might help, too.

2 Now open up that kit and make sure yours has all the parts that the box says are supposed to be in there. Lay them out on the sink or on the closed toilet lid so they are easy to reach as you are working.

3 Take off the tank's lid. Flush the toilet several times, to minimize the amount of water in the tank.

4 Absorb the rest of the water with a sponge. This last step is important because when you remove the fill valve there will be an opening in the bottom of the tank—whatever water remains will drain out and create a mess.

5 From underneath the tank, disconnect the water supply line at the tank. Using your pliers, remove the nut underneath the tank that is holding the fill valve in place. If it is an old toilet with rusted nuts you may need some lubricating spray.

6 Disconnect the chairn on the flushing arm from the rubber flapper at the bottom of the tank.

7 You will notice that the plastic tube from the old fill valve is clipped to the overflow tube. Unclip this tube to release the old valve.

8 Inside the tank, your fill valve will also have a nut and washer at the base of the tube. Loosen the nut and lift the old fill valve out.

9 Unclip the flapper ...

10 Attach the refill tube to the side of the valve body. It is a very tight fit, so don't give up!

11 Look on the side of the fill valve body. There is a line that shows you the "critical level" mark. It is very important that this mark is 1" above the top of the overflow pipe. It is a standard plumbing code to ensure proper installation.

12 Put the fill valve down in the tank and measure across from the overflow pipe. If the critical level mark isn't 1" above the pipe you may have to cut the overflow pipe.

13 Our model actually is adjustable, so after measuring the difference in height, twist the bottom of the fill valve to achieve the necessary 1".

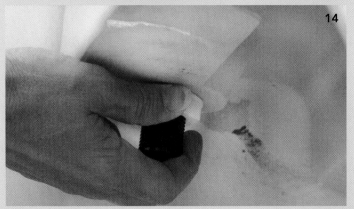

14 Set the fill valve into place down in the tank. Make sure the shank washer is firmly seated. Then, from underneath the tank, tighten down the locking nut on the valve shank securing it to the tank. Just don't over-tighten this nut as it may crack and cause your tank to leak! Yikes! Reattach the water supply line to the shank.

15 Back inside the tank, attach the refill tube to the overflow pipe using the angled clip. You can trim this tube if it is too long. We kept our original overflow pipe in place because it was working correctly.

16 We attached the new flapper to the overflow pipe. Make sure that your new one will seal the flush valve opening at the base of the overflow pipe if you are not replacing it. If it doesn't, you will have a leak causing your toilet to constantly run.

17 Take the chain that is connected to the flapper and attach it to the lever arm. You will have to tweak where to position the chain until you can raise the lever when flushing the toilet and the flapper is fully seated on the flush valve.

18 Make sure all your connections are tightened and then reach underneath to turn the shut-off valve back on to start

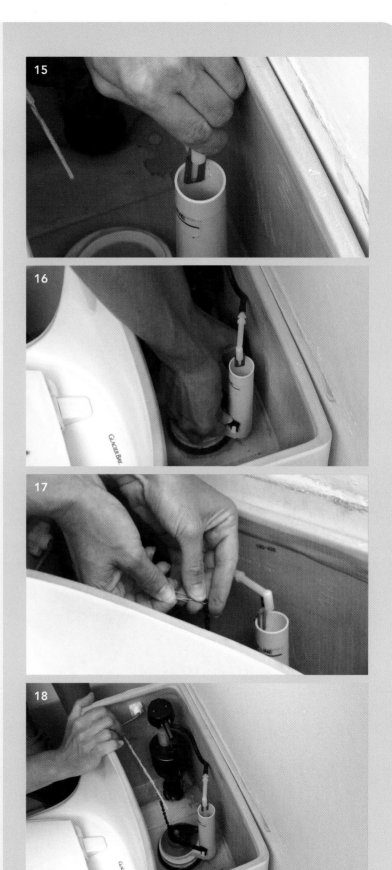

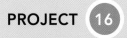

PROJECT **16**

REPLACE A TOILET HANDLE

HERE ARE A COUPLE OF THINGS to keep in mind when shopping for a new toilet lever. Check to see where the handle is located on the tank. Some are located in the front, some at an angle and some are on the side of the tank. The handle we are installing can accommodate any one of these locations. Also, less expensive handles have plastic parts, whereas the more expensive ones are made of metal. If you are trying to match your handle with the finish of your bath fixtures, they come in a variety of metal finishes as well.

Replace a Toilet Handle

TIME: 30 minutes

EFFORT LEVEL: Basic

TOOLS AND MATERIALS:
- Screwdriver
- Pliers
- Hacksaw (maybe)

INSTALLATION TIPS:
If you are installing a handle that has a metal lever arm, do not worry if the metal arm rests in water. Typically, the arm is made of non-corrosive material that is rust-resistant and will not damage your tank.

1 Start by removing the flapper chain or wire from the old lever arm. You may need to use a pair of needle nose pliers to loosen the clasp securing the chain.

2 Using pliers, remove the old shank nut. If yours is corroded and you are unable to remove it, use a hacksaw to cut it off.

3 Pull out the old handle and the lever arm through the mounting hole in the tank.

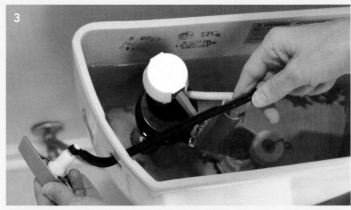

4 If your handle needs to be assembled, follow the manufacturer's directions ... we chose the chrome finish with the white handle accent.

5 Insert the handle into the tank mounting hole.

6 From inside the tank, attach the rubber or plastic gasket onto the handle stem.

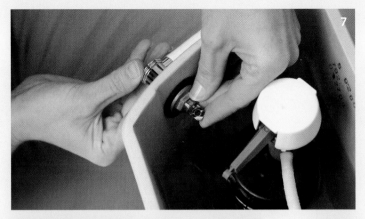

7 Thread the metal or plastic shank nut onto the handle stem and tighten down.

8 If your handle has the lever arm already attached, proceed to step 9. If not, then using the screw, lock washer and wing nut, attach the lever arm to the handle stem to secure it, but don't tighten it just yet.

9 Take the flapper chain or wire and align it straight with the lever arm. If you find that the lever arm is too long for your application, you will need to remove the lever and using your hack saw, make the necessary cut to shorten it. Insert the chain or wire clip on the lever arm.

10 Hand-tighten the wing nut that secures the lever arm to the handle stem. Test the handle by flushing the toilet. If the flapper fails to seal properly over the flush valve seat or the chain doesn't lift the flapper completely up, you will need to use another hole in the lever arm.

REPLACE A TOILET SEAT

I CAN REMEMBER AS A KID THOSE COLD, heavy toilet seats. Seems like it never failed that over time, they would get chipped or cracked just by accidently letting go of the lid too soon. "Don't bang the lid!" still echoes in my head. Then came along the fancy, soft and cushy ones…my memory conjures up a pink one my grandparents had…boy had they arrived! Those faded out, but having a more durable, comfortable toilet seat was here to stay. You can still find those cushy ones, while some are "elongated" now for more comfort. Depending on the style of your bathroom, you can also find wooden ones, colored ones, and in our case, one to match the "cottagey" feel that has the look of bead board on the lid. You can even jazz it up a bit by picking one that had a metal finish to match the metal fixtures in your bath. Who knew there would be so many choices for a toilet seat!

Toilet Seat

TIME: Less than 30 minutes

EFFORT LEVEL: Basic

TOOLS AND MATERIALS:
- Screwdriver
- Pliers

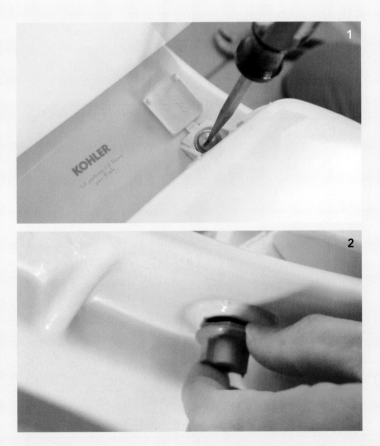

1 Depending on the style of your old lid, remove it by popping up the screw covers with a flathead screwdriver and unscrewing the screws that secure the lid to the toilet base.

2 If your lid doesn't have screws, use a pair of pliers to remove the locking nuts up under the toilet base that holds the lid in place.

3 With our new lid, we inserted each screw into the lid hangers.

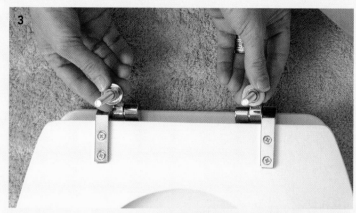

4 Slide a rubber, or plastic, washer onto each of the screws.

5 Holding the washers in place, carefully place the screws into the lid holes on the base of the toilet and align the lid evenly.

6 From underneath the toilet base, slide the washers and nuts on the screws and hand-tighten.

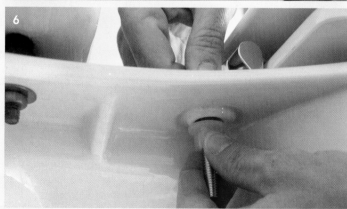

7 Once you made sure the seat is correctly aligned over the toilet base, tighten down the nuts to firmly secure the new seat.

Just adding something as simple as a new toilet seat and of course the handle we installed earlier, has jazzed up our bathroom nicely and inexpensively. Notice how our toilet seat now matches the bead board around our tub and cabinet doors. Sharky, our cat, is very impressed!

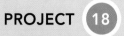

REPLACE A SHOWER HEAD

THESE DAYS, NO MATTER WHERE YOU look in the home improvement industry, everyone is pushing for a more lavish bathroom. Steam showers, body massage sprayers, therapy tubs; the list goes on and on. But what can you do if your budget just doesn't allow for all these great spa amenities? Well, we're going to show you one easy upgrade that will add that "spa" touch to your shower, but the first 6 steps of this showerhead installation can be used to replace any type of standard showerhead.

PLUMBING

Shower Head

TIME: Less than 30 minutes

EFFORT LEVEL: Basic

TOOLS AND MATERIALS:
- Screwdriver
- Adjustable wrench
- Cloth
- Teflon tape

1 If you are going to keep the existing shower arm, then leave it in place. With an adjustable wrench, loosen the nut on the showerhead and remove it. If there is old Teflon tape or plumber's putty, clean that away.

2 If you want to replace your shower arm, then firmly grip the showerhead and arm and twist off. You may have to use a wrench to loosen it. Don't be surprised if a bit of water comes out of the line, it's normal.

3 On your new arm you will notice that there is a long side and a short side. The longer side goes into the pipe inside the shower wall. Wrap that end with Teflon tape but don't let it fold over into the hole, it will block your water from flowing.

4 When you insert the arm into the water line in the wall you will be turning it clock-wise, so here's a tip about that Teflon tape: when you wrap it around the threads, wrap it in a clock-wise direction. That way when you twist it in place the fold at the end of the tape will press against itself sealing it up as opposed to being unwrapped and getting shredded.

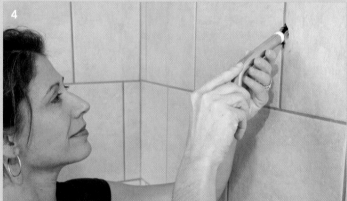

5 Before I go any further, I take the time to turn the shower lever on to double check my seal at the shower arm. If there's a leak I won't have to undo all my hard work to fix the seal with more Teflon tape.

6 Next, slide on the decorative arm cap that covers the hole in the shower wall. Keep in mind that some showerheads do not include a decorative cap in their packaging. Check to make sure you have one before you walk out of that hardware store.

If you are going to replace just the single showerhead, jump all the way down to step 18. If you're doing the fancy-smancy spa showerhead like ours, then read on to see how easy it is.

7 Our setup comes with a stationary and a hand-held showerhead. The hand-held head can slides up and down a bar. Assemble the slide bar with the bar clamp exposed and the bottom dome cap underneath it.

8 Out from the wall about ½", place the bar clamp under the shower arm and slide the bottom dome cap up to the arm. Set the upper dome cap on the shower arm and tighten it down into the bottom dome cap. Don't over-tighten.

9 The bottom of the slide bar is secured to the shower wall with a suction cup. However, our wall mount location fell on the grout line and it was an uneven surface. So we added adhesive backing.

10 Slide the wall mount on the bottom of the slide bar and leave about a 2" space at the bottom. Make sure the slide bar is plumb, press the wall mount firmly to the shower wall to create a tight seal. (Let the adhesive backing dry for 12 hours before you take a shower.)

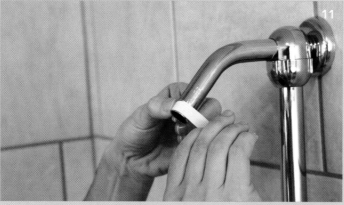

11 Take your Teflon tape and wrap the threaded end of the shower arm with it in a clock-wise direction. Don't cover that hole with the tape or you'll reduce your water pressure.

12 Install the shower diverter by twisting the nut onto the shower arm. Hold the diverter body firmly to ensure that it remains straight and level.

13 A good tip for tightening the nut on the diverter or even on your showerhead is to place a towel over the nut and use your wrench or pliers to tighten it down. Again, don't over-tighten it.

14 With your Teflon tape in hand, wrap both threaded ends on the diverter. One will be for the showerhead and one will be for the hand-held shower hose.

15 Place the rubber seal inside the shower hose fitting of the hex nut end. Make sure it is firmly seated in the bottom before attaching it to the diverter.

16 Tighten down the hex nut. This nut will tighten in the counter-clockwise direction, so adjust your Teflon tape accordingly. Tighten with a wrench or a pair of pliers.

17 On the tapered end of the shower hose, insert the rubber seal and attach it to the hand-held showerhead. Again, this tapered end tightens counter-clockwise, so wrap the Teflon tape counter-clockwise on the end of that showerhead.

18 Back up at the shower arm, you are ready to install your new showerhead! Place the rubber seal inside the showerhead nut and in a clock-wise direction, tighten down your showerhead. Wrap the nut with a towel to tighten it down with a wrench or a pair of pliers. Tah-dah! You are done!

HOW TO CAULK A TUB

AN OUNCE OF PREVENTION IS WORTH A pound of cure. And when it comes to your caulking, nothing could be truer. Hundreds of pounds of water go into a bathtub and then it drains out. This causes heavy flexing and requires a caulking (also called sealant) that is pliable. Plus, all your tubs and sinks need silicone caulking compound to prevent cracks and gaps from popping up wherever the tub or sink meet the wall or surface.

It's no surprise that wherever tubs and sinks meet walls, tiles and countertops water becomes your enemy. A wet environment creates moisture, mildew and attracts dirt. All of which can damage the joint, and cost you some serious cash if you don't keep these areas well maintained. Anytime you begin to see cracking or pealing caulk, get out the caulk gun, it's time to replace it.

Caulk a Tub

TIME: About 30 minutes

EFFORT LEVEL: Basic

TOOLS AND MATERIALS:
- Tub and tile cleaner
- Flatheard screwdriver, grout scraper or chisel
- Cloth
- Scissors
- Silicone caulk and caulking gun

1 This is an example of a caulking job that should be redone. Lumpy, inconsistent and in some areas, not even covering the gap. Step one, we've determined the problem...

2 Use the screwdriver or whichever tool you feel works best for removing the old caulking. Once started, you can remove large strips of caulking by hand. If you're scraping grout, you'll tackle it with the screwdriver, or better yet, there are a variety of good grout removal tools. Just make certain you don't scratch or mar the sink or tub. Using a caulk remover helps because it breaks down the caulk making it easier to get up.

3 Once your old caulking is completely removed, it's important to thoroughly clean up any mildew or dirt. The new caulking needs to adhere to a clean surface or your time and effort will go to waste. Pour denatured alcohol in a small cup and with a clean cloth, wipe down the surface area where you will be using the caulk.

4 Grab your new caulk tube and your caulk gun. Remove the cap and with a utility knife, trim off the end of the nozzle. Some fancy caulk guns have a tip cutter in the handle.

5 Now I like to start out with a smaller hole in the tip of the nozzle. There is nothing worse than having too big a hole which will create fatter beads of caulk. This leads to too much caulk being dispensed at once and can create a huge mess to clean up.

6 I also like to cut the tip of the nozzle at an angle. This gives me better control over the direction of the bead as I am applying it in the cracks.

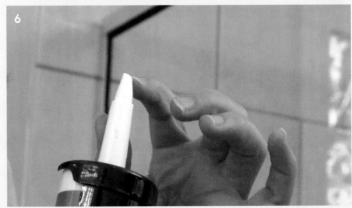

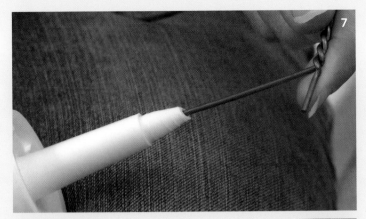

7 Once you have the tip of the nozzle just the way you want it, you will need to puncture the inner seal of the caulking tube. Again, most caulk guns have a thin wire attached to the front end of the gun for this purpose. If yours doesn't, you can use a wire coat hanger.

8 Some folks say they don't want to take the time to tape off the surrounding surface when they are caulking. I like to tape off the sides of the wall or tub surround so I can avoid more cleanup at the end. I will say this, silicone sealant can be a *bear* to clean up on tiles and grout lines, so use that tape!

9 With a firm and steady hand, start at one end and work your way down the length of tub, trying not to pause. Again, use the angle of the nozzle to help you work the caulk into the gaps and move the bead along so it doesn't clump up.

10 With my finger dipped in water, I lightly ran it across the caulking bead to smoothen it out. That is why the tape is very helpful! You could also tape the side of the tub if you accidentally cut the nozzle too big and will have a large bead of caulk to work with.

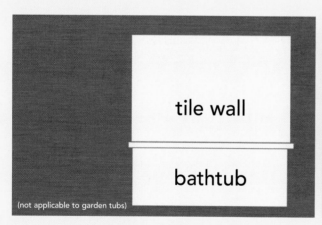

Re-caulk
a tub

11 Once you have a smooth bead of caulk, peal up the masking tape. Be careful to pull the tape straight up from the horizontal surfaces or straight out from the vertical surfaces. This will ensure that your bead has a nice edge.

12 Give your caulking a good 24 hours of drying time before you use your tub, especially if your tub is a shower/tub combination. Once it's dry you are ready to enjoy!

tile wall

bathtub

(not applicable to garden tubs)

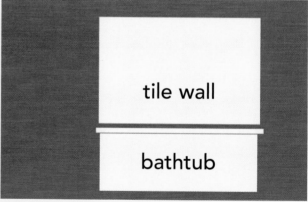

tile wall

bathtub

When you're caulking a tub, you need to be aware of what the weight of the water (when the tub is filled) will do to the gap between the tile on the wall and the tub itself. As you fill the tub with water, the tub will settle, or sink a bit, pulling away from the bottom edge of the tile. This is natural and nothing to worry about, but it is something to consider when caulking. If you caulk the wall edge of the tub while empty, the gap will be smaller, and when the tub is filled with water, the caulk may separate and gap. The clever approach is to fill the tub with water to create the gap that will occur when the tub is full. Then go ahead and caulk, letting the caulk dry before emptying the tub. The caulk's elasticity will allow it to squeeze smaller as the gap closes, but re-expand the next time the tub is filled!

Other Bath & Shower Tips

CAULKING TIPS

• To make sure you don't squeeze out too much caulk while applying it, cut the tip of the tube at the first joint marked on the tip. If the gap is bigger than your bead of caulk, trim the tip a little more. The worst thing you can do is cut the tip too big...it will create a huge mess when you go back and use your finger to smooth it out.

• Since the caulking gun is already out, go ahead and seal any opening where fixtures come through the wall.

• Depending on the number and size of your sealing projects you can purchase toothpaste-size tubes or tubes that fit in a caulking gun. Drying times vary, some take 48 hours or more, thus spacing out multiple sealing projects over time is prudent so that you always have a usable shower or sink.

• For re-caulking the base of a tub, shower or sink follow the same steps.

• Save your remaining caulk by placing a galvanized nail in the tip of the caulk tube. Wrap some tape around it to seal the opening. The caulking will remain usable for a few months.

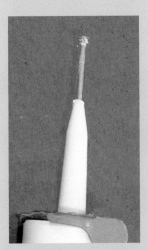

TUB LEAKS

Depending on where your leak is coming from, tub leaks can be simple to fix or, sadly, a bear to fix. If your spout is leaking water, check to see which handle, hot or cold, is not turning off completely. Then, simply shut off the water at the meter box and remove the handle that needs repair. Usually all that is needed is a new O-ring due to wear and tear of the old one.

If you have a leak from the plumbing of your tub, this is where it can get tricky. If you can access the plumbing from a panel on one side of the tub or from underneath in the basement or crawl space, you are in great shape to replace the drain fittings or just tighten them down. If you don't have access to your tub's plumbing you are going to have to create one. If your tub backs up to a closet or another room, or has a ceiling under it and you can see water stains, cutting into the drywall sounds hazardous, but honestly cutting and patching drywall to fix this issue is a small price to pay if left unattended. Most leaks can be fixed by just replacing the drain fittings. A good tip is take your old piping with you to the hardware store to make sure you get the exact fit for your new one.

4 WALLS, FLOORS & CEILINGS

Nothing captures the personality of your home better than the walls, floors and ceilings. Think about it. You can create atmosphere galore with your fancy furniture and your swanky knickknacks. The tone of the room, however, radiates in the soothing shade or electric shock of color splashed across your walls, the warmth and texture found on your floors, and the clean lines of your ceiling. Maintaining all of these things that literally surround you, is important to having a beautiful, inviting and happy home. Start with your walls.

Popping Nails and Screws

From time to time you may run into popped nails or screws that haven't been driven into the wall all the way or they are starting to make their way out due to your house shifting over time. If a screw pops out, most times just setting your variable speed drill in a low drive and tightening down the screw should secure it back into place. The best solution for popped nails is to pull them out and replace them with drywall screws. This ensures that your drywall is securely fastened. You will need to countersink the screw head just below the surface of the drywall, but not too deeply. I have had the variable speed setting up too high on my power drill before and screwed the drywall screws in so quickly they shot straight through the drywall into the stud. After you set the screws below the surface you will need to spackle the dimple left by the nail head and sand it smooth once it dries. If you nail pop happens on a ceiling like the one pictured here (textured), read below for help hiding the fix.

Fixing Textured Ceilings

Drywall is the same material that is used to create your ceilings. It's hung the exact same way as your walls, just a bit trickier since you are working above your head. Joint compound, paper joint tape and drywall screws are all used to give your ceiling a smooth, clean finish. But what if you have a textured ceiling? Repairing those types of ceilings are not as easy as 1-2-3, like patching holes in a smooth surface. Well, I shouldn't say they're not a snap to repair, because they are. You might have to spend a bit more time working on the desired effect of your repair to make sure it matches. But all is not lost if you don't feel you possess the artist's hand ... here's a quick and easy way to fix those holes and no one should be the wiser.

The first thing you'll need to do is pick up some all-purpose drywall compound. Lightly sand the area you need to repair and fill the hole with the compound. Let it dry. In a tray, dilute some joint compound with just a bit of water. You want to slightly thin its thickness. This will make it easier to "shape" your texture. You can pick up a texturing paint brush at your local hardware store. If you want to create your own, grab one of your paint brushes and cut the bristles in half crosswise. I would make sure this is a cheaper brush and one you don't mind losing to your ceiling cause. Dip the brush into the slightly thinned joint compound and begin dabbing it on the repair to create your texture. Have a putty knife or broad knife on hand to take off any of the textured tips that might be too long so they will be even with the texture already there. Let it dry and then prime and paint it. If you have serious doubts about your texturing ability, don't despair! There are spray cans of different textured finishes that you can use to match your ceiling. They can be a bit pricey, but are very effective.

REPAIR DRYWALL HOLES

MY DAD INTRODUCED ME TO DRYWALL REPAIR AS A YOUNG BOY OF NINE years old. My little brother and I decided to lineup 10 soda can "pins" down in the basement and create our own bowling alley. Dad's bowling ball bag inspired the idea as we hefted the heavy ball over to the bowling lane. Juvenile enthusiasm and competitiveness took over as the ball hurtled to the makeshift pins.

At some point, I remember a sinking feeling that something bad was about to happen. I was right. The ball smashed through the pins and set itself halfway through the wall. Needless to say, Dad was not happy and diligently guided me through the steps in drywall repair.

Hopefully your repairs are not caused by such foolishness. However, sooner or later you will face some sort of drywall repair caused by numerous scenarios:

- missing a nail and puncturing the wall with a hammer
- moving the new couch into the house, crunch! the leg gouges the wall
- cracks in the ceiling or walls from a settling house
- old nail holes whenever you move or redecorate

Accidents happen and walls need fixing. Thankfully, repairing walls is a straightforward process.

These projects will focus on simple drywall repairs that address the unsightliness of a "holey" wall or ceiling. Each application below can be applied to your ceiling, just check its thickness which usually differs from the wall thickness when using a patch to repair larger holes.

Drywall Holes

TIME: 10 minutes to a couple of hours (drying time)

EFFORT LEVEL: Basic

TOOLS AND MATERIALS:
- Drop cloth
- Putty knife
- Spackling paste
- 220-grit sandpaper
- Primer, paint and paintbrush

TIPS Spackling paste "sinks" into the hole as it dries, that is why you need to have a little mound of it right over the hole.

Depending on how deep the hole is, like double-layered drywall or plaster, you may have to apply a few layers of spackling, drying and sanding in between each layer, to achieve your desired results

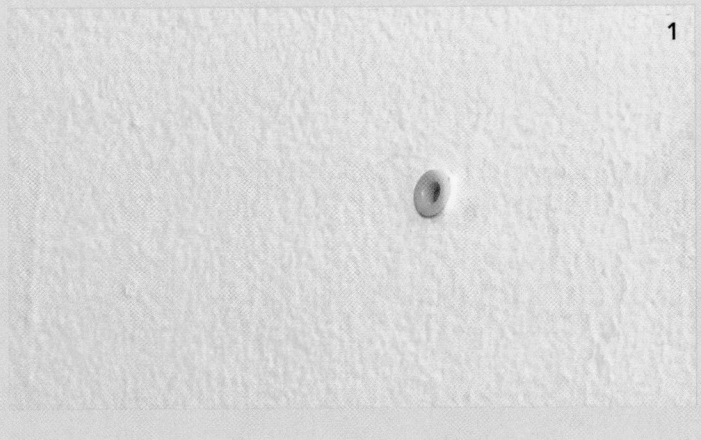

1 One of the most common drywall repairs is patching the wall after removing a plastic anchor, like the one shown here.

2 Using a pair of needle nose pliers, gently pull the anchor from the wall. Sometimes anchors are so well installed that you can't pull them out, so the next best option is to actually push them through.

3 If you can pull out the anchor, chances are there will be shredded drywall paper around the edges. You can try to push them into the hole, but the best way to deal with them is to sand them smooth.

4 Using a glob of spackle on your finger, cover the hole using a generous amount of the spackle to leave a little mound.

5 If you apply the spackle with a putty knife, you will run the risk of scraping off too much as you apply it, which will leave a dimple in the hole.

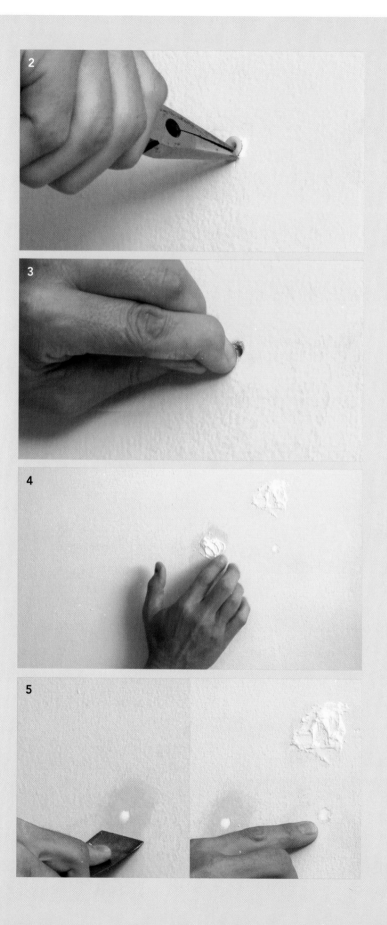

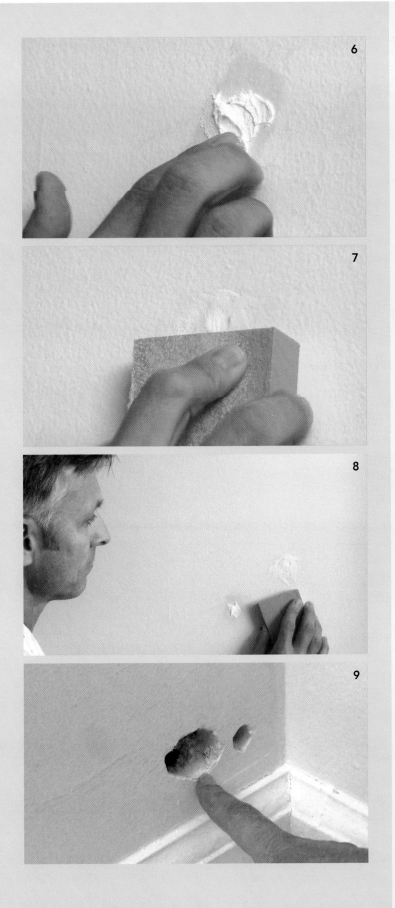

6 Go back over these with your fingertip full of spackle. Once your spackle starts to dry, it will shrink and may leave an indentation where the hole is. A mound of spackle will settle into the hole perfectly as it dries.

7 Once the spackle has dried, take a piece of fine-grit sand paper (220 should do it) or a sanding block and sand the surface.

8 Take wide, broad strokes with your sanding block or paper to make sure the surface of the wall and the spackle are level and uniform. A good tip is to prime the spackled area before you paint, so there won't be a reflective sheen where the spackle was sanded.

9 If your hole is bigger than an inch, then you can repair it with the following steps. You will need to pick up some fiberglass mesh tape, drywall (joint) compound and tray, a sanding block, a putty knife and a 4" taping knife. This hole was created when Steve ran some cable wires through a half wall in our downstairs media room. It's a mess now and needs to be repaired.

10 Grab a small tub of all-purpose joint compound for these types of repairs; you should also have a pair of scissors to cut the mesh tape.

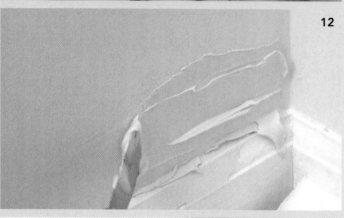

11 On the clean and dry surface of your wall, cut off a piece of mesh tape large enough to extend past the repair area by ½" on each side and press it into place.

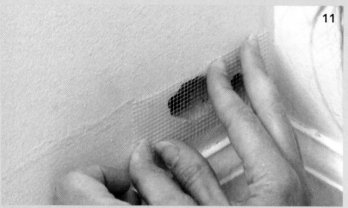

12 With your putty knife, apply the joint compound over the mesh tape, coving it completely. Don't worry right now if it is uneven or lumpy.

13 If you are working near your base boards, door or window trim, take a lint-free cloth and wipe the excess away before it has time to set up and dry.

TIP Use an old cloth to remove mud from trim.

TIP If you are repairing an indentation or crack that is too shallow to fill in with the drywall compound, use the utility knife to provide enough depth. Cut away any rough paper edges.

14 With your 4" broad knife (taping knife), gently take an angled swipe across the layer of joint compound. Try not to pause in the middle of going from one side to the next. You want your joint compound to be even, smooth, and completely covering the mesh tape. I try to spread the compound about a good three inches past the mesh tape edges so I can "feather" out the compound evenly with my taping knife.

15 Once the joint compound has completely dried, take your sanding block and working from the middle of the area to the outer edges. Sand down the compound until it's completely smooth and blended with the wall surface.

16 Wipe away the drywall dust and with your putty knife apply another coat of joint compound to the first layer. Make sure that you cover all the first layer with your second coat.

17 Feather it out again with your 4" taping knife and let it dry. Once it has completely dried take your sanding block and sand down the compound until it is completely smooth and flush with the surrounding wall area. Now you are ready to prime and paint!

 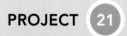
REPLACE BROKEN FLOOR TILE

TILE LOOKS GREAT, IT HOLDS UP TO ABUSE, and it occasionally can crack. Replacing tile is much more simple than it seems ... the most difficult part is finding matching tile if you don't have any replacements on hand.

Replace Broken Tile

TIME: Less than 30 minutes

EFFORT LEVEL: Basic

TOOLS AND MATERIALS:
- Safety glasses
- Power tool with grout removal attachment
- Hammer
- Cold chisel
- Towel
- New tile
- Tile adhesive
- Putty knife
- Notched trowel
- Tile spacers
- Grout
- Grout float
- Sponge
- Grout sealer

TIPS Be sure to remove all the thin-set underneath the old tile. Failure to do this could lead to cracking again due to weight on the uneven surface below the tile.

When removing cracked tile, keep your eye out for water damage. If you notice moisture, dampness, mold or mildew, beware. This indicates water damage and simply replacing the damaged tile will be fruitless. You need to discover where the damage is coming from and assess the scope of damage and effort of repair. If it is extensive, consider calling a professional tiling contractor.

1 A tile doesn't need to be broken into pieces to be unsightly. As houses settle, tile can crack along stress lines, leaving an unattractive presence on your floor.

2 With your safety goggles on, remove the grout so none of the surrounding tiles are damaged. Use a hand power tool with an attachment to remove grout or simply use a grout saw.

3 Lay the towel or a cloth over the damaged tile. Grab a hammer and break the tile into smaller pieces. Remove the pieces of tile.

4 As you can see, when breaking a tile, the material basically shatters into tiny bits. You might want to wear a pair of gloves to protect your hands, but you certainly need to protect your eyes because those broken bits will get airborne!

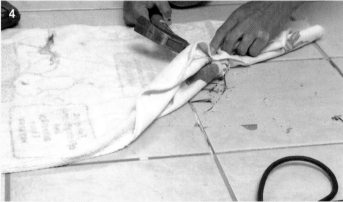

5 Using the chisel and hammer carefully remove the old tile adhesive from the floor. Avoid gouging the floor. Vacuum the remaining small pieces and dirt.

6 A clean, smooth sub-floor is absolutely key to ensure a lasting repair. So remove all that old thin-set. You can use a hand-held power tool like ours or you can use a cold chisel and a hammer to chip away the old adhesive. Whatever method you use, you have got to get the area all cleaned out.

7 If you have a small area to repair, use a putty knife to "butter" the backs of the replacement tiles with adhesive. In our case, we have a large enough area to accommodate a notched trowel to spread our adhesive.

8 You can purchase thin-set in a bag and mix it yourself with water on the job site. We like to use premixed adhesive because it is easy and convenient to use. Pop open the lid, stir it up with your putty knife or margin trowel and you are ready to start spreading in place.

9 At a 45° angle, spread the thin-set evenly over your sub-floor. You want nice and even grooves in the thin-set and you don't want to see any of the sub-floor underneath after you have finished spreading it.

10 Before you set your tiles in place, go around the edges with your putty knife or margin trowel to clean up any excess thin-set that has built up. If you don't, this might cause you some grouting headaches down the road.

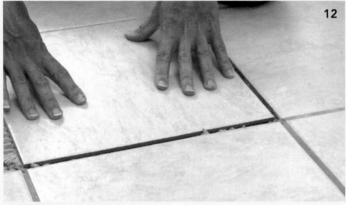

11 With tile in hand, gently lay the tile down in the thin-set. Make sure that it is exactly where you want it. If you set it in the thin-set and then change your mind, you will have to pry it up and re-spread the thin-set in that area and scrape the thin-set off the back of the tile before you can set it again. Hassle!

12 Once it's seated in the thin-set, gently press it down until it is level with the surrounding tile height. It's a good idea to even twist the tile back and forth in small motions to get it to settle down into the adhesive.

13 Come back with your putty knife or margin trowel and once again get out all the thin-set that has oozed up into the tile joints. If you let it stay there, your grout will have no where to go once you start applying it.

14 Use your spacers to evenly space your grout lines all the way around the tiles. We put at least two on each side of the tile. Another good use of the spacers is to use them to clean the thin-set out of your grout lines.

15 Once you have all your tiles in place and evenly spaced with the other tiles, use a 4' level or other straight-edge, to double check the height of your new tiles with the height of the existing tiles.

16 Give your thin-set about 18 hours to set up. Some manufacturers say 24 hours, just read your thin-set label. Then mix your grout according the manufacturer's directions and pour it into the grout lines.

17 Use your rubber float and work at a 45° angle across the tiles, working the grout down into the grout lines. You can use your putty knife or margin trowel to take up any of the excess grout. Just make sure the grout lines are filled up completely.

TIP Scoop up large excess with trowel.

18 With a damp sponge, gently wipe off the excess grout that is on top of the tiles. Very carefully wipe **across** the grout lines, (not straight down them). Over-wiping them will pull the grout right out of the joints and you will have to fill them again. After about 30 minutes, the tiles will start to haze over. Take the sponge and wipe just the tiles again, staying away from the grout lines. Once the grout is dry, apply a good grout sealer and you are done!

5 DOORS & WINDOWS

When I am asked about the best place to start in getting a house ready for spring or fall, I immediately suggest the doors and windows. There's no faster way to waste your hard-earned cash than by letting it seep out in the gaps that form around these places over time. Every house will settle in its foundation, and over time, weather can break down the exterior sealant rendering it ineffective.

Safety in your doors and windows is an important factor, too. It's always a good idea to inspect the locks and deadbolts, making sure the screws are securely fastened and there are no broken components to either.

While the trouble shooting projects in this section primarily focus on doors, weatherproofing your windows and double checking their security is just as important and just as easy.

When I was planning the renovation of our home, checking out the latest and greatest on doors and windows was no simple task. With so many styles and brands to choose from, it was overwhelming. The decision making process was impacted by several factors: 1) the aesthetic aspect—it had to fit the style of the new home, 2) we wanted energy efficient doors and windows and 3) we had to stay in our budget.

Doors are big-ticket items. If you've ever had to replace one, you know even one isn't cheap. Maintaining them is another story. With just a few simple projects you can increase the life span of each, not to mention save some serious dough on your monthly power bills.

Door and Window Maintenance

As part of our season maintenance, we always inspect the exterior wear and tear on the doors and windows. So much of our heated and cooled air can escape each year and that means a lot of wasted money and energy. Simple checks to make sure there are no drafts can greatly reduce the waste. If it's drafty, weatherize it!

Another area we always pay close attention to is the exterior trim and surface of the doors and windows. Depending on what yours are made from, it's important to troubleshoot any fading, blistering, warping, or peeling of paint on the doors or windows. If the weather is beating them up pretty badly, its going to be only a matter of time before it's time to replace them.

Our front entryway door is solid wood that is protected by a covered porch. However, we keep a close eye on the top coat, the polyurethane, to make sure it hasn't started to break down with time. If yours is exposed to direct sun, you will have to be vigilant to ensure your door is continually protected because sunlight can shorten the life span of the top coating.

Aluminum-clad doors and windows will certainly fair the best from exposure to the elements, but you want to make sure that they are sealed properly and scratch or dent free … rust will be your enemy in that situation.

Vinyl construction is another option for doors and windows, just be aware that over time, you might encounter blistering or cracking.

Keeping a fresh coat of paint on both your doors and your windows will add to the protection. It can be a daunting task to undertake ever so often, but well worth the sweat equity to having beautiful and long-lasting doors and windows.

Weather Proofing—Replacing the Weather Stripping for Your Door

Weather stripping doors and windows is an easy and beneficial energy-saving project for your home. Weather stripping is available in several types: foam or felt, vinyl, and metal. The least expensive types are made of foam or felt.

Foam stripping has an adhesive backing that makes installing them a snap.

Felt stripping is held in place with staples or glue.

Both foam and felt stripping are inexpensive, however over time they tend to break down or wear out. If you have doors or windows that aren't opened and closed frequently, is a suitable option. Foam stripping can withstand moisture, whereas felt cannot.

Another type of weather stripping is called vinyl gasket.

Nowadays most new doors and windows have this type of stripping factory installed. It is a great choice due to its durability and resistance to moisture. It is available at home improvement stores and is a little more expensive than foam or felt.

INSTALL WEATHERSTRIPPING

RISING ENERGY COSTS NEVER SEEM TO go down, only up. Research shows that a tiny crack around a door is roughly the equivalent of a 6-inch hole in your door. The U.S. Department of Energy states you can save 10% on your heating and cooling bill by reducing the air leaks in your home, doors and windows. The D.O.E. suggests using an incense stick to locate air leaks on a windy day — finally a practical use for incense sticks.

Weather stripping doors and windows is an easy and beneficial energy-saving project for your home. Steve and I are going to show several different styles of weatherstripping in this project, and even though the materials might be different, the process is still the same regardless if yours is vinyl, metal or foam.

Install Weatherstripping

TIME: About 30 minutes

EFFORT LEVEL: Basic

TOOLS AND MATERIALS:
- Weatherstripping kit (usually includes screws)
- Tape measure
- Marker
- Scissors
- Hacksaw

1 As with any repair work, for weatherstripping you have got to get rid of the old, damaged stuff first. Either pull or pry off any existing weatherstripping. Wear gloves if you are dealing with any kind of metal weatherstripping.

2 With your measuring tape, measure from the bottom of the door frame to the top corner on both sides. Don't take your top measurement yet. You will do that in a minute.

3 With your weatherstripping laid out, transfer the measurements you have for both sides onto the two long, side pieces.

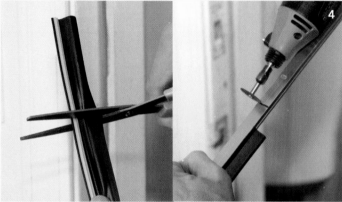

4 Cut the pieces to length using a pair of scissors, (for vinyl or foam stripping), or a hacksaw or hand-held power tool, if you are installing metal stripping.

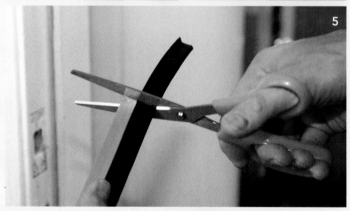

5 If you trimmed your metal piece with a hacksaw or power tool, you will have to come back and trim off the excess fiber stripping with a pair of scissors.

6 Then gently realign the two ends so your stripping will create a nice, tight seal when in place.

7 Once you have your side pieces measured and cut, install them by starting at the top and either push them into the doorframe groove, like this …

8 … or using the screws provided with your weatherstripping, screw them into the doorframe …

9 … or by holding the small brad nails with a pair of needle nose pliers and hammering them gently into the doorframe.

10 Once both sides are in place, you're ready to take the measurement for the top piece. Measure from the weatherstripping in place on one side to the other piece of weatherstripping.

11 Now you can install the top piece of weatherstripping either by pushing it into place or attaching it with the screws or nails provided.

12 If you installed the metal weatherstripping, you will need to use a putty knife or a 5-in-1 tool to gently pry out the edge next to the door stop. This creates the necessary V-groove to keep air from escaping around your door.

That's Steve below, wistfully thinking of all the money he's saving by upgrading his weatherstripping. Sometimes it's the little things that mean a lot!

PROJECT (23)

CAULKING A DOOR FRAME

DOORS

Caulking

TIME: 30 to 45 minutes

EFFORT LEVEL: Basic

TOOLS AND MATERIALS:
- Exterior grade caulk
- Caulking gun
- Painter's tape
- Wiping cloth
- Mineral spirits

ONE SUREFIRE WAY TO KEEP THOSE ENERGY PRICES DOWN IS to ensure that the air you are heating or cooling stays right where it needs to be … inside your house. If you're going to take the time to weather seal your door and window openings, then the next logical step is to caulk around the sides of both where they meet the siding of your house. Even the tiniest of cracks can be the escape route to the outside. Like my mom always said to us kids, "What do you want to do, heat the neighborhood?"

1 Before you start, you want to inspect the cracks around your door to make sure caulk will fill the gap. If your cracks are larger than say $3/8$", a good tip would be to fill those with something like oakum, which is just plain 'ol jute rope you can pick up at the hardware store. Also, you want to make sure that the area you are caulking is nice and dry, clean of dirt and debris.

2 Start by taping off the wall of the house. I like to use painters tape, because it keeps the caulk only where you want it. If you are caulking against a surface like brick, it can be tricky.

3 I apply a second piece of painter's tape to the door frame to keep things as tidy as possible. I hate cleaning up messy caulk.

4 Cut the tip of your caulking tube to the desired thickness you want your caulking to be. Try not to make it too wide or you'll have a big mess on your hands.

5 Pierce the inner seal of the tube with a sharp object, like a long nail. Some caulking guns have both a cutter at the handle for the tip and a wire for piercing the tube.

6 With a slow and steady motion, start at the top and run a nice consistent bead of sealant down the side of the door. If air escapes the tube while you are pushing it out, it will leave a gap. Just go back to where the gap started and pick up from there.

7 I like everything to be nice and tidy and make sure there are no holes in my caulking, so I wet my finger with water ...

8 ... and smoothed out the bead, working from top to bottom. This is where the tape comes in handy. If my bead is too thick, I will have a buildup of caulking pretty quickly that will spill over onto the tape and not my siding. This step is optional if your bead looks like it has completely sealed the gaps.

9 Gently pull off the tape before the caulking starts to dry and clean up stray caulk with mineral spirits.

10 Here's a good little tip to remember when removing that painter's tape: as you are pulling it away from the house, work slowly and always pull the tape at an angle, away from the bead of caulking. This creates a more blended edge of the caulk to your siding and there is no "lip" on your nice, new bead of sealant."

REPLACE A DOOR KNOB

CHANGING OUT A DOOR HANDLE IS VERY easy and surprisingly, very rewarding. If you need to change a lock for security reasons, learning how to do this can set your mind at ease. You'll find, too, that sometimes it's cheaper to change the entire door locking system itself than to pay a locksmith about $60 to rekey an existing one. Whether you are changing an interior door or one on your exterior door, the mechanics of it all are pretty straight forward. If you are installing a door knob on a new door, you will need to cut the holes for the handle and the latch. We highly recommend you invest in a handle installation kit. It comes with both hole saws, the 1" and the 2⅛", and it also has a sturdy template you can attach to your door to ensure proper location and spacing. It even adjusts to the varied thicknesses of a door. Follow the instructions that come with the kit and you will be a pro at setting up the door for the steps below.

Replace a Door Knob

TIME: Less than 1 hour

EFFORT LEVEL: Basic

TOOLS AND MATERIALS:
- Screwdriver
- Hammer
- Hole saw kit, if necessary

1 With your screwdriver, remove the screws on the inside collar of the door handle to release the knobs on both side of the door.

2 Gently pull out the interior door handle or knob to expose the inner latch and spindle.

3 Remove the exterior handle or knob, making sure the spindle comes off still attached to the handle and not remaining in the latch body inside the door cavity.

4 Using your screwdriver, remove the two screws securing the faceplate of the latch to the side of the door.

5 Pull out the latch from inside the door cavity. Most times it will just come right out, but if it doesn't, use a flathead screwdriver and insert it into the pin hole and push it out. If you are saving all the parts of the old handle, try not to force the latch out as it may break it.

6 Slide in the new latch body making sure that the beveled face of the latch plunger is facing the door jamb. You make need to use a hammer and a block of wood to seat it into the door cavity. Secure the new latch faceplate with the screws provided.

7 With the new exterior handle or knob in hand, line up the spindle with the large hole in the latch body.

8 Push the handle flush with the door, making sure the spindle is extended all the way through to the other side of the door.

9 Line up the interior handle with the spindle. This can be a bit tricky, so hold not only the exterior handle securely to the door, but put your thumb on the latch to steady it as well.

10 Once you have the interior handle pushed in and both handles are flush to the sides of the door, insert the two long mounting screws to the interior handle collar and tighten down.

11 On the doorjamb itself, remove the old strike plate and inspect the surrounding wood frame. You may need to shave or hollow out the existing hole to accommodate the new strike plate.

12 With the screws provided, attach the new strike plate the doorjamb. Test the door to make sure the beveled latch plunger aligns to the strike plate and springs completely into place in the strike plate hole.

FACEPLATE TIPS

Your new handle set will have two options for your latch faceplate. One will have squared corners and one will have rounded corners. Most manufacturers will have the square one already installed on your faceplate, because it is the most common style in use. However, if your original faceplate was mortised for a rounded one, you will have to pry off the squared one with a flathead screwdriver and attach the rounded one. It should snap on, but sometimes you may have to use a pair of pliers to pop it into place.

REPLACE A DEAD BOLT

Replace a Dead Bolt

TIME: Less than 1 hour

EFFORT LEVEL: Intermediate

TOOLS AND MATERIALS:
- Screwdrivers — Flat head and Phillips
- Hammer
- Hole saw kit

AS WE SUGGESTED WITH THE DOOR HANDLE REPLACE-ment, if you are installing a dead bolt on a new door, which is a project, it is worth the investment to purchase a hole saw kit to make sure the holes are aligned correctly and evenly. The kit will have the two hole saws, 1" and the 2⅛", and the template for positioning on the door and on the door jamb for the strike box. Follow those instructions to prepare your door for the steps below.

1 Using a screwdriver, remove the screws holding the old dead bolt mechanism from the inside of the door.

2 Gently pull the interior section of the thumbturn unit away ...

3 ...revealing the deadbolt latch inside the door cavity.

4 The outside cylinder unit will simply pull away from the deadbolt latch without having to remove any screws.

5 With your screwdriver, remove the two screws securing the latch faceplate to the side of the door.

6 Pull out the deadbolt latch. Now you may have to use a flathead screwdriver to pry it from the door cavity. They have been known to get stuck. If you plan to reuse the old deadbolt, be careful not to force it out too hard or you might damage the inner workings of the latch and basically ruin it.

7 If you'll notice, our old latch faceplate had square corners, but was covering up rounded mortised edges on the door. So, we pried the square cornered one off our new latch and snapped on the rounded one to fit our existing edge better. With the deadbolt retracted, slide the new deadbolt latch into the door cavity and secure it with the two screws provided in your kit.

8 Insert the exterior cylinder unit into the deadbolt latch body making sure that the round pin fits into the correct backset slot (either 2⅜" or 2¾") and that flat driver bar is underneath the latch.

9 With the thumbturn of the interior side straight up, slide into place making sure the drive bar goes into the drive slot of the interior side. If installed correctly, these two pieces should stay in place without your support.

10 Insert the two long screws that came with your kit and tighten them down to firmly secure both sides together.

11 Now it's time to test your hard work! Turn the thumbturn to the outer edge of the door. If the deadbolt engages and operates smoothly, you have done a great job! If the bolt drags while turning the thumbturn, loosen the screws and check the horizontal alignment of the interior and exterior cylinder units.

12 Over on the doorjamb, install the new strike box. This strike box is a metal chamber that completely encases the bolt once it is engaged. This is the best defense against any intruder because these bad boys are hard to kick out of place if anyone tried to. Get one if your kit doesn't supply it.

13 Attach the strike plate faceplate. Again, yours may either be squared or rounded on the edges, so install the one that is right for you.

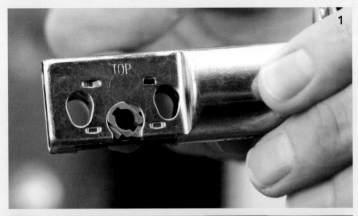

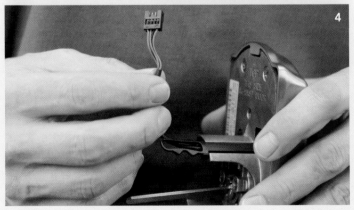

COMBINATION LOCK

We felt that having a combination to unlock the front door would make it easier for family and guests to come in and we wouldn't have to worry about a hidden key getting discovered or misplaced. Installation for this type of deadbolt is pretty much the same as the standard as far as prepping the door and door jamb if it's a new door. Also, inserting the latch body is the same, making sure you choose the correct latch faceplate for your door and the deadbolt is retracted into the latch body.

1 Installation of the dead-bolt latch is the same. With either make sure you can read the word "TOP" correctly and not upside down when you are ready to install it in the door cavity.

2 Slide the new deadbolt latch into the door cavity. You may have to gently tap it into place using a hammer and block of wood over the latch to protect it from damage.

3 With the two screws provided, secure the dead-bolt latch to the side of the door. You may have to pry off the square cornered faceplate if you have a rounded one. Just snap on the right one for your application before you install the latch. *Retract the deadbolt* before you move on to the next step.

4 Inspect the exterior keypad assembly. You will see the cable that powers the lighted keypad on the outside. Below that, you will have a bar, or cam, used to activate the deadbolt.

5 With the exterior side of the keypad assembly, slide it into place making sure that the cables pass over the top of the deadbolt and the cam passes through the center of the deadbolt latch.

6 Install the inside mounting plate with the two screws that are provided. Make sure that the cable comes out of the plate at the hole near the top and that the cam comes out the center hole of the mounting plate and is pointing down.

7 Install the battery that is included and connect the cable from the mounting plate to the cable of the battery wiring. Route and tuck all the cables around the battery.

8 Attach the thumbturn plate with the two long screws included. Make sure that the thumbturn is pointed away from the door edge before installing the screws and tightening them down.

9 Test the thumbturn to make sure it is turning smoothly and completely into place in the strike plate on the doorjamb.

10 Now you are ready to follow the manufacturers instructions on how to program and create your combination to lock and unlock your new deadbolt!

JODI'S HONEY-DO LIST

- ☐ Remove screens from windows and install storm windows.
- ☐ Clean out gutters and downspouts.
- ☐ Insulate pipes in your home's crawl spaces and attic.
- ☐ Store firewood at least 30 feet away from your home.
- ☐ Clean the clothes dryer exhaust duct, damper and space under the dryer.
- ☐ Make sure all electrical holiday decorations have tight connections.
- ☐ Check the attic for adequate ventilation.
- ☐ Clean the kitchen exhaust hood and air filter.
- ☐ Check the water hoses on the clothes washer, refrigerator icemaker and dishwasher for cracks and bubbles.
- ☐ Test all ground-fault-circuit-interrupter (GFCI) outlets.
- ☐ Check your home for water leaks, especially your water heater.
- ☐ Have your HVAC serviced once in the spring for your air conditioning unit and once in the fall for your heating unit.
- ☐ Replace your furnace filter.

- [ ] If storing your lawn equipment for the winter, empty all gas-powered lawn equipment of fuel and oil.
- [ ] Test your emergency generator.
- [ ] Have a certified chimney sweep inspect and clean the flues and check your fireplace damper.
- [ ] Remove bird nests from chimney flues and outdoor electrical fixtures.
- [ ] Inspect and clean dust from the covers of your smoke and carbon monoxide alarms and replace batteries.
- [ ] Make sure the caulking around doors and windows is adequate to reduce heat/cooling loss.
- [ ] Make sure that the caulking around your bathroom fixtures is adequate to prevent water from seeping into the sub-flooring.
- [ ] Trim your trees and remove dead branches.
- [ ] Maintain your steps and handrails.
- [ ] Repair broken stairs and banisters.
- [ ] Inspect your roof.
- [ ] Check and change the filters on your in-home water filtration system.
- [ ] Check to make sure you have fresh batteries in your emergency flashlight and radio.

Suppliers

3M
3M Center
St. Paul, MN 55144-1000
(888) 364-3577)
solutions.3m.com
Abrasives

AMERICAN STANDARD
1 Centennial Plaza
Piscataway, NJ 08855-6820
800-442-1902
www.americanstandard-us.com
Plumbing fixtures

DAP PRODUCTS INC.
2400 Boston Street
Suite 200
Baltimore, MD 21224 GE
(800) 543-3840
www.dap.com
Sealants

DELTA FAUCET COMPANY
55 E. 111th Street
Indianapolis, IN 46280
(800) 345-3358
www.deltafaucet.com
Faucets

FEIN POWER TOOLS
1030 Alcon Street
Pittsburgh, PA 15220
(800) 441-9878
www.feinus.com
Power Tools

FLUIDMASTER
30800 Rancho Viejo Road
San Juan Capistrano, CA 92675
(949) 728-2000
www.fluidmaster.com
Toilet Repair

FROST KING -THERMWELL PRODUCTS
420 Route 17 South
Mahwah, NJ 07430
(800) 526-5265
www.frostking.com
Insulation

GARDNER BENDER
PO Box 3241
Milwaukee, WI 53201-3241
(800) 624-4320
www.gardnerbender.com
Electrical/wire management tools and testers

GE SEALANTS AND ADHESIVES
9930 Kincey Ave.
Huntersville, NC 28078
(866) 275-4372
www.geadvancedmaterials.com
Sealants

HUNTER FAN COMPANY
7130 Goodlett Farms Parkway,
Suite 400
Memphis, TN 38016
(888) 830-1326
www.hunterfan.com
Ceiling Fans

THE HOME DEPOT
2455 Paces Ferry Rd. NW
Atlanta, GA 30339
800-430-3376 (U.S.)
800-628-0525 (Canada)
www.homedepot.com
Tools, supplies and hardware

INSINKERATOR
4700 21st Street
Racine,WI 53406
(800) 558-5700
www.insinkerator
Disposers

IRWIN INDUSTRIAL TOOL COMPANY
92 Grant Street
Wilmington, OH 45177-0829
(800) 464-7946
www.irwin.com
Hand tools

KLEIN TOOLS, INC.
450 Bond Street
PO Box 1418
Lincolnshire, IL 60069-1418
(800) 553-4676
www.kleintools.com
Hand tools and electrical testers

KOHLER
444 Highland Drive
Kohler, WI 53044
(800) 456-4537
www.us.kohler.com
Plumbing

LOWE'S COMPANIES, INC.
P.O. Box 1111
North Wilkesboro, NC 28656
800-445-6937
www.lowes.com
Tools, supplies and hardware

LEVITON MFG. COMPANY INC.
59-25 Little Neck Pkwy.
Little Neck, NY 11362-2591
(800) 323.8920
www.leviton.com
Lighting and controls

LUTRON
7200 Suter Rd
Coopersburg, PA 18036-1299
(888) 588.7661
www.lutron.com
Lighting and controls

MAPEI
1144 E. Newport Center Drive
Deerfield Beach, FL 33442
(800) 426-2734
www.mapei.us
Flooring

MOEN INCORPORATED
25300 Al Moen Drive
North Olmsted, OH 44070
(800) 289-6636
www.moen.com
Plumbing fixtures

PRICE PFISTER, INC.
19701 DaVinci
Lake Forest, CA 92610
(800) 732-8238
www.pricepfister.com
Faucets

PROGRESSIVE LIGHTING
625 Braselton Parkway
Braselton GA 30517
(613) 822-6800
www.progressivelighting.com
Lighting

SCHLAGE LOCK COMPANY
2119 E Kansas City Rd
Olathe, KS 66061
(888) 805-9837
www.schlage.com
Locks

STANLEY TOOLS PRODUCT GROUP
480 Myrtle Street
New Britain, CT 06053
(800) 262-2161
www.stanleytools.com
Hand tools

MORE GREAT TITLES FROM
POPULAR WOODWORKING AND BETTERWAY BOOKS!

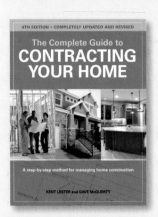

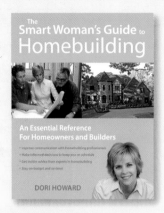

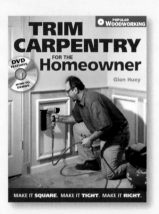

**THE COMPLETE GUIDE TO CONTRACTING
YOUR HOME - 4TH EDITION**

By Kent Lester & Dave McGuerty

This step-by-step guide to managing the
construction of your own home is jamb
packed with:
- To-do check lists for each phase of the
  construction process
- Hundreds of illustrations that clearly show
  what the author is teaching you
- Pages and pages of each necessary form
  you'll need to complete your home project

ISBN 13: 978-1-55870-871-6
ISBN 10: 1-55870-871-5
paperback, 320 p., #Z3040

**THE SMART WOMAN'S GUIDE
TO HOMEBUILDING**

By Dori Howard

Using the information in this book, you can:
- Improve your communication with
  homebuilding professionals
- Make informed decisions to keep you on
  schedule
- Get insider advice from experts in
  homebuilding
- Stay on budget and on time!

ISBN 13: 978-1-55870-817-4
ISBN 10: 1-55870-817-0
paperback, 160 p., #Z1027

TRIM CARPENTRY FOR THE HOMEOWNER

By Glen Huey

Master carpenter Glen Huey shows you:
- How to use ready-made supplies and
  materials from home center stores
- How to install or replace door, window, chair
  moulding and other room trims
- How to make and trim out fireplace
  surrounds and mantles
- How to install wainscotting and built-in
  furniture

ISBN 13: 978-1-55870-814-3
ISBN 10: 1-55870-814-6
paperback with DVD, 128 p., #Z0953

These and other great woodworking books are available at your
local bookstore, woodworking stores, or from online suppliers.

www.popularwoodworking.com

Easy to Use
Compatible with both Mac and PC, the
disc contains live-action demonstrations
and instructions showing how to perform
the ten most common household upgrades
and repairs.

FIX IT IN A FLASH
10 Most Common Fixes
Bonus DVD Table of Contents

**Watch Jodi and Steve tackle these projects in video,
with extra tips and tricks for each project:**

- Unclog a Drain
- Fix a Running Toilet
- Repair a Leaky Facuet
- Recaulk a Bathtub
- Change an Outlet

- Install a Dimmer Switch
- Replace a Light Fixture
- Re-wire an Old Lamp
- Repair Holes in Drywall
- Replace Broken Tile